101 Questions & Answers on the Crusades and the Inquisition

DISPUTED QUESTIONS

John Vidmar, OP

Paulist Press
New York / Mahwah, NJ

Cover images, clockwise from top left: Red Cross by ManuelVelasco/iStockphoto. com; Armor by Tomasz Bidermann / Shutterstock.com; Dark hallway by kinlem/ iStockphoto.com; Iron Maiden by pandapaw/Shutterstock.com; Wheel by Vlad Kol/iStockphoto.com; Torture chair by Syldavia/iStockphoto.com; Fighting Knight by Litvin Leonid / Shutterstock.com; Crusaders by wynnter/iStockphoto. com; and Crusader Arches by Lokibaho/iStockphoto.com

Cover design by Sharyn Banks
Book design by Lynn Else

Library of Congress Cataloging-in-Publication Data

Vidmar, John.
    101 questions & answers on the crusades and the inquisition : disputed questions in the history of Christianity / John Vidmar.
        pages cm
    Includes bibliographical references.
    ISBN 978-0-8091-4804-2 (alk. paper) — ISBN 978-1-58768-083-0
    1. Church history—Middle Ages, 600-1500—Miscellanea. 2. Crusades— Miscellanea. 3. Church history—16th century—Miscellanea. 4. Inquisition— Spain—Miscellanea. I. Title. II. Title: One hundred one questions and answers on the crusades and the inquisition.
    BR162.3.V53 2013
    270—dc23
                                                        2013005420

ISBN: 978-0-8091-4804-2 (paperback)
ISBN: 978-1-58768-083-0 (e-book)

Published by Paulist Press
997 Macarthur Boulevard
Mahwah, New Jersey 07430

www.paulistpress.com

Printed and bound in the
United States of America

Contents

THE 101 QUESTIONS AND ANSWERS

The Crusades

Preface

To put the Crusades and Inquisition together in one book may seem a bit strange. First, what do these two historical events have to do with each other? Second, they both seem to be embarrassing moments in the Church's history. Why bother to revisit such terrible times? When I told friends I was working on this book, they almost uniformly said, "Good luck on *that* one."

Yet the Crusades and Inquisition have a *lot* to do with each other. For one thing, in both cases, crusading or military activity was followed by an inquisition or legal activity; thus, the Medieval Inquisition followed the formal Crusades of the period 1096–1291 and the Spanish Inquisition followed the Reconquista of Spain (eleventh century to 1492). I believe that this was no accident and that the various Inquisitions were extensions of the Crusades; they served as relatively peaceful, legal means of continuing the ideals and purposes of the violence or military activity that had preceded them. In the case of the Albigensian Crusade, I believe that the Inquisition was instituted precisely to end the indiscriminate violence that was taking place in southern France. Similarly, the Spanish Inquisition (and its spin-offs) followed on the heels of the Reconquista that resulted in the expulsion of the Muslims from Spain in 1492. It was established to carry on legally what the Spanish conquerors, or *conquistadores*, had effected militarily.

Furthermore, neither the Crusades nor the Inquisitions are the invariably embarrassing moments in the history of the Catholic Church that they have been painted to be. The Crusades as well as the Inquisitions have been caricatured and misrepresented in ways that are only recently being reexamined and corrected. In fact, much like the revision of the English Reformation going on in historical circles, the rewriting of the Crusades and Inquisitions, engaged in by people of different faiths, is fascinating and enlightening. It is my hope that this book will introduce the reader to a period of history that is not only interesting but is now being treated far more accurately than it has ever been before. I hope also that this book will address the most common questions posed about these disputed movements, introduce the reader to the most current research, and permit the reader to realize that neither movement is as simple as it has been commonly depicted, nor as unrelated to the other as has been thought.

The Crusades

1. Much has been written about the Crusades and other military campaigns launched in the Middle Ages by Christians against Muslims or heretics. On the one hand, my impression is that the Christian military was doing something heroic in trying to preserve Europe and the Holy Land for orthodox Christians. On the other hand, I've read that the Christians committed great atrocities during these campaigns. Can you define what these military campaigns were?

There were three:

1. The Crusades were a series of eight formal military operations inaugurated by European Christian nations and directed at freeing the Holy Land, and specifically Jerusalem, from the control of the Muslims. They began in 1096 and ended in 1291, when the port of Acre (Jerusalem's port city at the time) fell to the Muslims.

2. The Albigensian Crusade was an attempt by the northern French to subdue the rebellious southern French, who were led by the Albigensians (Cathar heretics who were centered in the city of Albi). This crusade would prove to be the bridge between the violence of warfare and a new age of litigation against opponents of orthodox Christianity. The Inquisition, as this era of litigation was known, was begun both to end the "pyromania" of the crusade in France and to continue the ideal of enforcing adherence to Christianity by less violent means.

3. The Reconquista was the attempt by the Spanish to take back their land from the Muslims, who had conquered it in 711. This was a protracted effort that lasted from the eleventh century until 1492, when the last Muslim strong-

hold of Granada fell to the Spanish Christians. The Reconquista experienced several bursts of activity, followed by years of truce or inaction. Most of the military activity increased dramatically in the thirteenth century and would end long after the Crusades to the Holy Land and the Albigensian Crusade had ended; hence its place as third in the list of military actions.

2. Jerusalem was taken over by the Arabs in 638. Why did the crusaders wait so long to mount a rescue attempt?

There are many reasons. For one thing, Europeans had problems of their own with internal warfare, fending off Muslim invasions into Spain and France in the eighth century, Viking and Magyar invasions in the ninth and tenth centuries, a lack of political organization, and so forth. While Charles Martel stemmed the Muslim incursion into France with his decisive victory at Tours in 732, Charlemagne's impressive kingdom (771–814), which built on this victory, fell apart when he died. It was divided among his three sons, who did not get along with each other and who lacked their father's vision of a united Europe.

The Vikings were quick to fill the vacuum, invading Britain from Norway and Sweden in the late eighth century. Monasteries were especially vulnerable as they were in remote locations along seacoasts and were essentially defenseless. Vikings attacked Lindisfarne in northeast England in 793 (the monks would eventually relocate to Durham) and Iona in 806, when sixty-eight monks were slaughtered in what is now known as "Martyrs' Bay." These incursions were stopped by Alfred the Great in 878 at Edington and by the French king, who in 911 granted the Vikings land along the mouth of the Seine River; this land became known as Normandy, or the "Land of the Norsemen."

Following on this, the Magyars were being pushed out of Hungary by invading Tatars in the late ninth century and made incursions into Germany until Otto I (the Holy Roman Emperor) defeated them decisively at Lechfeld in Bavaria in 955. They never posed a threat to European peace again. But the combination of the Viking and Magyar invasions distracted the Europeans from forming what would later become an imposing political unity. In addition, the original Muslim conquerors of Jerusalem were Arabs, who tended to be moderate victors. Although they placed some restrictions on Christians—for example, the imposition of taxes and special clothing, the elimination of images and most public worship, and so forth—the Christian population coexisted peacefully with these Arabs, and pilgrimages by Christian foreigners were permitted. But in the early 1000s Muslim Turks, who were and are not Arabs, had taken over Jerusalem and, under Caliph Hakim, had begun a ten-year pogrom of Christians, restricting their movement, mandating the wearing of distinctive clothing, confiscating Church property, burning crosses, and building small mosques on the roofs of Christian churches. In 1009, Hakim ordered the destruction of the Church of the Holy Sepulchre in Jerusalem, and, by 1014, some thirty thousand Christian churches had been burned, pillaged, or transformed into mosques.

Christian pilgrims to the Holy Land now found themselves harassed by the Turks, and reports and rumors of beatings, robberies, and molestations began to filter back to Europe, creating an atmosphere of collective outrage.[1] Philip Jenkins, in his *Lost History of Christianity*, soberly details the tensions rising during the eleventh century with the advent of Turkish power. The Christian bastion of Melitene was destroyed by a Turkish army in 1057 and its population massacred.[2] Nor was this an isolated incident. While Pope Urban II may have exaggerated recent outrages as "propaganda" in his speech at Clermont in November 1095, which sparked what later became known as the First Crusade (see QQ. 10–13), he did not have to invent the seriousness of the overall situation. A military response now had an urgency it had not had before.

3. I've heard that the pope had another agenda in desiring a crusade to the Holy Land at this time. Did he wish to accomplish more than freeing the holy places for Christian worship?

Several popes, going back to Gregory VII, envisioned a crusade as a way of reuniting the western and eastern Christian Churches, which in 1054 had been rent asunder by schism. Gregory even pictured himself as personally leading the crusade to the east, with a diplomatic mission to Constantinople in mind.

The pope had still other reasons for wanting to start a crusade. He wanted to assert his authority over that of the secular kings and bring them to a common project; only *he* was really capable of doing this. The kings of England and France and the emperor of Germany were all in a state of excommunication and did not trust one another. The Holy Roman Emperor, angry at the new papal policy directed against his control over appointments to the papacy, had imposed an anti-pope during the tenure of Pope Gregory VII in 1080, forcing Gregory to flee to Monte Cassino and eventually Salerno, where he died in 1085. The French king, Philip I (1060–1108), was living in an adulterous marriage. King William II of England would not recognize Urban II until years after he was crowned pope. So the pope was looking for something that would bring these kings back into the fold but would also give them a common purpose. A crusade would be a way of freeing them from the penalty of excommunication and uniting them in fighting a non-Christian enemy, something that, he hoped, would take them away from fighting one another.[3]

4. It is often said that the nobility of Europe wanted to give their younger sons something to do, and the Crusades provided a perfect format for these sons to prove themselves, earn glory, riches, and land, and get them away from their fathers' domains. Did this happen?

It seems not. This is one of the "myths" of the Crusades. In most of the crusades it was the father who went, not the sons. In the First Crusade, none of the kings went—they were still under excommunication—rather, the major players were heads of families, risking their fortunes and properties, and this remained true throughout. In subsequent crusades, we see the kings Richard the Lionheart of England, Philip II of France, and the emperor Frederick Barbarossa of Germany, and later Louis IX, who is known today as St. Louis, spearheading the crusading effort. Younger sons were not the leaders, although they had an important part to play, but money and land were not the principal objects of the crusade.[4] Many people who were wealthy landowners lost a lot of money.

5. Did the crusaders have to commit to going on this crusade in any way? For example, did they have to take an oath or sign up for the duration?

Crusaders were volunteers who were first vetted by their parish priests, who wanted to make sure that only the best Christians were committing to the crusade. Thus, any people who would have wanted to take advantage of the opportunities afforded by a crusade for less honorable reasons—thieves, especially—would have been barred from going.

Next, the crusader swore an oath that pledged him to the enterprise from start to finish, with a penalty of excommunication if he deserted. This was to ensure the success of the crusade and also to guarantee the holy nature of the commitment. This was to be a "holy war" in the best sense of the word.

6. But how can war be "holy"?

G. K. Chesterton (1874–1936), possibly the most influential English Catholic writer of the twentieth century, wrote in his typically paradoxical style that "the only just war is a holy war." That sounds almost crazy to us in the twenty-first century, especially in light of the rhetoric surrounding *jihad*. But what Chesterton meant was that the only reason we can justly go to war is to defend something that is holy, such as our family. We should never go to war over a trade agreement or a boundary dispute. But when someone attacks our family, then we can do what we need to do to protect that sacred thing. That applies on a national basis as well. Christians in the eleventh century believed that the Christian family was being assaulted in Jerusalem.

In addition, a massive revival of religion was taking place in Europe. Not only monastic life benefited—laypeople wanted to join in this religious enthusiasm as well. Many felt that Christianity had a birthright to possess the holy places, and one solution was to retake Jerusalem.[5] The crusaders were not going to the East in order to force Muslims to convert to Christianity, but to free the pilgrim routes to the holy places.

7. When did this armed pilgrimage get the name *crusade*?

The names *crosata* and *croseria* do not appear until the late twelfth and thirteenth centuries. Those who went were then called *crocesignati*, that is, "those signed with the Cross," or crusaders.[6] Originally it was not looked on as a war in the sense that World War II was conceived, but as an "armed pilgrimage."

8. Can you define what, exactly, is meant by a pilgrimage?

Pilgrimages are journeys taken to sacred places in order to honor the persons buried there, or the events that occurred there, in order to expiate one's own sins or simply to pay tribute to the people involved. In some cases, pilgrimages are taken in search of healing, both physical and spiritual.[7]

While there is some archaeological evidence (graffiti, for example, and remnants of shrines) that the tombs of Peter and Paul were visited by pilgrims as early as the second century, the earliest references to pilgrimages in Christianity date from about the fourth century, when Christians expressed a desire to see the Holy Land and places where Christ was born, lived, preached, suffered, and died.[8] Constantine's mother, Helena, made a great deal of going to the ruins of Jerusalem in the early fourth century and recovering relics of Christ's life. Not unexpectedly, Rome came next, because people wished to venerate the sites associated with Sts. Peter and Paul and other early Christian martyrs. Several of these are still venerated today, such as the Scala Sancta (or Holy Stairs) in Rome near the Lateran Cathedral, reputedly the stairs that Christ ascended to his trial with Pontius Pilate.

In the Middle Ages, during the crusade period, other sacred places gained renown. These included Compostela, Spain (the supposed burial place of St. James the Apostle); Vezelay, France (associated with the bones of Mary Magdalene); the cathedral of Cologne, Germany (the shrine reputedly containing the bones of the Three Kings); St. Cuthbert's monastery in Lindisfarne, England; and others.[9] But even minor shrines and monasteries (St. Foy in France, for example) had a revered saint to pray to. Journeying to them was difficult and was regarded as penitential. The arduous journeys were rewarded by a communal sense of faith and by the satisfaction of praying at the site of the shrine, beseeching the saint to pray on one's behalf.

The Crusades were an extension of this movement, but obviously with an edge. The pilgrims wanted to go to Jerusalem, but with the purpose of ensuring that Jerusalem would be truly accessible to future pilgrims. In order to do that, they needed to take some weapons.

9. Did these crusaders have a symbol?

The red cross was devised to represent the crusade. It consisted of a large red cross in the center, surrounded by four crosses: the Jerusalem Cross. It signified the five wounds of Jesus: the nails that pierced his hands, his feet, and his side. Another cross was the

Maltese Cross, which was also red. When the First Crusade was first preached in Clermont by Urban II in 1095, excitement was so widespread that red material ran out, and people demanded to be tattooed with the red cross. To this day Muslims are uncomfortable with the notion of the Red Cross as a relief agency and prefer to name their comparable organization the "Red Crescent." Descendants of crusading religious orders, such as the Knights of the Holy Sepulchre, still use the Jerusalem Cross as an emblem to this day.

10. Who were the first to go off on crusade?

Before the First Crusade was organized by professional soldiers, enthusiasm for defending the Holy Places propelled a ragtag army that consisted of the poorly armed and poorly led faithful, led by a charismatic preacher named Peter the Hermit—only one quarter of his "army" consisted of fighting men. His attempt, known as the People's Crusade, was a considerable disaster. It rambled through Germany and Hungary, fighting Jews (when they could be found) and other native populations over scarce resources. The animosity of these crusaders toward Jews was so great that it distracted them from their main purpose. Solomon Bar Simson, a member of the Jewish community in Mainz, described in 1140 the attacks on Jewish communities in Germany, sometimes borrowing from older material. Often, the Jews fled to the bishop's enclave, where they were promised protection by the bishop, who sincerely opposed the crusading rabble. But when the bishop himself was faced with execution, he sometimes fled, leaving the Jews to fend for themselves. Later, as the more disciplined armies trod through the same territory, the persecution was lessened, but even here Solomon claims that "Godfrey of Boullion, may his bones be ground to dust," continued in the spirit of the People's Crusade, "vowing to go on this journey only after avenging the blood of the crucified one by shedding Jewish blood."[10] It must be said that St. Bernard of Clairvaux tried heroically to prevent such anti-Jewish behavior in subsequent crusades and was summoned by the archbishop of Mainz to denounce a hot-headed monk named Raoul, who thought that the logical first step of a crusade was the killing of Jews. Even as early as the 1130s, before the calling of the Second Crusade, Bernard was preaching against the injustices done to the Jews, saying that the Jews were "the apple of God's eye," so that the Jews of the Rhineland considered him a "righteous Gentile."

When the People's Crusade arrived in Hungary, they brawled with the natives and left four thousand dead. They sacked the city of Belgrade, the population of which had fled in their wake. The emperor in Constantinople was nervous about their presence and lack of discipline in the area but, after cautioning them to wait for the real armies not far behind them, shuttled them over to Asia Minor, where they were massacred by the Turks. Only two thousand to three thousand of the estimated forty thousand survived, including Peter the Hermit, who would join the next crusade.

Despite its disastrous outcome, however, the People's Crusade served a purpose: it lulled the Turks into thinking that they had defeated their principal opponent, and they got back to fighting each other, not realizing that the greatest military expedition in human history was headed right in their direction.

As time went on, the camp followers and families were told to stay home, and the professional soldiers pressed on.

11. What were these professional armies like?

The armies that were organized by the lords of Europe (no kings or emperors went on this First Crusade; see Q. 4) were made up of knights, who were heavily armored and rode large Belgian workhorses, which were also heavily armored.[11] The knights were professional soldiers, but they would be assisted by a platoon of five to ten foot soldiers, who would assist the knight in mounting and dismounting and would use him as a shield, much like patrols used tanks during World War II.

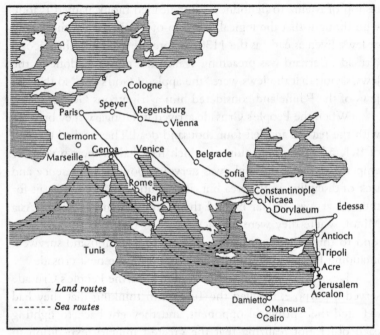

MAP 1: THE CRUSADES

12. How large were these armies?

The First Crusade had four main armies, amounting to nearly seventy thousand soldiers. Whether or not the army of the Persians that attacked Greece at the Battle of Thermopylae in the fifth century BC (estimated at 150,000 troops) or the army of Alexander the Great as he headed toward India (estimated at 37,000 troops) was as large as this, it was certainly the largest army the West had seen in many centuries. (The Norman army that successfully attacked Britain in 1066 under William the Conqueror was probably closer to fifteen thousand at most.) They went by different routes (see map 1), with the goal of assembling together at Constantinople in August 1096. In fact, the first troops did not arrive until late December 1096, and the rest followed in April and May 1097.

13. How did the western generals coordinate their marches and tactics?

Not particularly well. There was no supreme commander in the sense that General Dwight D. Eisenhower functioned as one during World War II. The closest thing the crusaders had to a "father figure" was Bishop Adhemer of Le Puy in France, who had been appointed by the pope to go along with the crusaders in his place. Bishop Adhemer was not a military leader but was assigned to assure the "religious" goal of the crusade. He seems to have been popular and effective in doing this, but he would die during the siege of Antioch (see QQ. 17–18). His presence would be missed.

The generals realized in the beginning that each would need to take a different road to Constantinople in order to avoid running into one another's armies, but also to maximize the food supplies along the way. Once the fighting began, however, and its consequent takeover of land, relations between the generals and the armies became more strained. At each juncture, the various generals needed to negotiate who would do the fighting, who would be in support, and so forth. In the long run, this lack of a central leadership was the undoing of the crusading movement. General vied against general; even military religious orders competed against each other (see QQ. 26–29).

The initial enthusiasm of the crusading movement overcame this during the First Crusade, at least until the troops overcame and occupied Antioch (see Q. 17). There the infighting turned poisonous and nearly ruined the crusade.

14. How did the Greek emperor take to the presence of so many western soldiers in his domain?

Alexius Comnenus (c. 1048–1118) was, to say the least, considerably uncomfortable with the presence of the westerners, especially the presence of the Normans who had inhabited his land in southern Italy and Sicily and effectively eliminated any Greek usage in the liturgy—which was the immediate cause of the rift between the eastern and western Christian Churches and which remains a point of diplomatic negotiation to this day—and who would just as soon attack Constantinople as they would the Turks. He wanted to move them on as soon as possible.[12]

Alexius I also had different ideas about what this "crusade" would accomplish. He wanted to restore the land of Asia Minor to the Greeks, while the westerners were not concerned about his empire. They had not come to help him retrieve his land; they had come to free the Holy Land. This would remain a major point of contention between the Christian generals.

15. When did the crusaders and the Turks first encounter each other?

The first exchange took place in May 1097 at Nicaea, a fortress town on the Roman road that led through Asia Minor. Fortresses would need to be captured before a major army could continue. Otherwise, they could always cause mischief with one's supply lines.

Nicaea was surprisingly (and deceptively) easy to take. The sultan and his army were away fighting other Turks, thinking they had taken care of the Christian army that was rumored to be coming his way. So his wife, the sultana, was in charge and, after six weeks of a siege—the standard method for reducing a fortress—surrendered to the crusaders. The surrender contained the seeds of dissension within the Christian ranks. Westerners viewed the siege as a challenge from the besieged fortress with the understanding that, if the walls were breached, there were virtually no rules against murder, rape, theft, and so forth. This, to some degree, was how soldiers were compensated. The Greeks, however, were more civilized and negotiated with the sultana on their own. (This, in itself, infuriated the western generals.) When the assault on the city walls was about to begin, the Greek flag was raised from the ramparts of the city, and the sultana surrendered to the Greeks, thus depriving the westerners of their plunder. Then the Greeks plied the sultana with gifts and sent her on her way, further bewildering the westerners whose knowledge of graciousness in victory still left a lot to be desired. Thereafter, the tension between the Greeks and the westerners would prove to be continuous and divisive.

16. After their initial success, what further adventures awaited the crusading armies?

After conquering Nicaea, the allied armies confidently marched along the Roman road toward Antioch—without the Greeks, who had headed east and north in hopes of restoring lost land. But shortly after, in July 1097, the westerners ran into the sultan of Nicaea's army, returning to lift the siege of his city. He was too late, but he surprised an army of Normans under the generalship of Bohemond, one of the more important Norman generals. Finding himself now in the vanguard, Bohemond hunkered down and waited for reinforcements, which he knew were behind him.

This was the first real encounter in the open field between enemy armies. Their ways of fighting were completely different, and both groups needed to learn how their opponent fought. The Turks were lightly armored, rode small and fast horses, and were given to hit-and-run tactics, while the westerners were heavily armored and rode large, ponderous horses, followed by packs of infantry. Each army needed to learn about the other and would do so on the battlefield. At this first Battle of Dorylaeum (see map 1), the westerners narrowly prevailed. They now had a clear path to Antioch, their next major obstacle.

17. Why was Antioch such a major obstacle? What happened there?

Antioch was the first major city encountered by the crusaders, who arrived there in October 1097. It had significant walls around it, and it protected the main road to Jerusalem. The crusaders needed to reduce it before they could move on. While Nicaea had been caught off guard and was unprepared for a siege, the people of Antioch knew exactly what to expect. They were prepared with provisions for a long siege. In addition, the walls of a city so large were porous, so that rations and even soldiers could be let in without being noticed. A siege of a city this large was a very difficult undertaking. Disease also took its toll among the besiegers.

It almost broke the crusaders. Almost eight months of siege were having no effect, the path to Jerusalem seemingly blocked, when an inhabitant of Antioch who was in command of a tower left open a gate on the southeastern side of the city.[13] The crusaders, primed for this eventuality, poured in, the Christian population of the city rose against the Muslims, and the city was taken.

18. The road to Jerusalem was now apparently open. Why didn't the crusaders press on?

The crusaders ran into two problems. First, Antioch, having been bled dry by the besiegers, was thus devoid of all resources—no food, no water. Second, now that the besiegers were inside the city, they became the besieged. A Turkish army led by the great Turkish general Kerbogha was now going to besiege the army that had formerly been the besiegers. The situation was so desperate that a western general, Stephen of St. Blois, fled the city and told a Greek army that was prepared to relieve the siege not to bother, because everyone would be dead by the time they got there. The Greeks held off, further confirming the westerners in their opinion that the Greeks were afraid of battle and were worthless as allies. Stephen would later regret his decision and go on pilgrimage again, partly to atone for his desertion.

Fortunately for the westerners in the besieged city, a lance was discovered by one of its soldiers, and word spread quickly that it was the "Holy Lance" that pierced Jesus's side on the cross. Morale soared, and the Norman general Bohemond challenged the Turkish general to a fight outside the city walls. Kerbogha foolishly thought that the western soldiers were so depressed and poorly equipped (they had eaten nearly all of their horses, after all) that victory was a sure thing, and so he agreed to let the Normans meet him in a fair fight. Bohemond prevailed.

Now, at last, the way to Jerusalem was clear, but strangely the crusader leadership did not seem eager to move on.

19. This seemed to be the perfect moment for the crusaders to press on, and yet the leadership hesitated. Why?

Not one single crusade leader wanted to continue. The armies were exhausted. Resupplying the army was going to take time, and the generals wanted to wait until they had sufficient provisions (and horses) to continue. They had been lucky to escape with their lives, their numbers were drastically reduced both because of the combination of their eight-month siege of Antioch (through disease) and the siege that they themselves had to endure under Kerbogha.

In addition, Bohemond, who was probably their most aggressive general, rather surprisingly did not want to go any further. He had defeated the Turks and considered himself the rightful ruler of Antioch, a significant prize indeed. Other generals had attempted or achieved the conquest of a large city and wanted to claim it as their own—such as the port of Tarsus or the frontier city of Edessa—and Bohemond did not want to be left behind in this "race" for material gain. He was, indeed, a lesser son with few prospects, and he regarded this conquest as his due. The Greeks, who had demanded that all reconquered property be returned to them, had failed to come to the aid of the westerners in besieged Antioch, and Bohemond regarded this as a betrayal of the agreement between the armies.

20. This seems to contradict what you said earlier about the material gains to be made from going on crusade. Why, when the crusaders were within reach of Jerusalem, would they suddenly start bickering over turf?

In Bohemond's case, he thought that he had risked everything, had taken the initiative, had won the battle, and stood to gain nothing unless he claimed Antioch—one of the traditional patriarchates of the Christian world. A previous arrangement with the Greeks, which specified that any land that had been recovered by the crusaders would revert to the Greek emperor, was considered to be forfeit in light of the Greek reluctance to aid in the battle for Antioch. Bohemond could always go to Jerusalem on pilgrimage, and he did eventually, but he stayed in Antioch to consolidate his victory.[14]

While the leadership quibbled over these matters, however, the rank-and-file soldiers were determined to march on to the final goal. They had not come this far merely to establish a Norman kingdom, and their motivation was still focused on the goal for which they had enlisted. And they wanted to go home. After a few months in Antioch, they forced the hand of the leaders by deciding to continue, whether the leaders wanted to go along or not. They were eager to get the job done and return home. About six thousand soldiers started off, and Raymond of St. Giles, the count of Toulouse (d. 1105), another one of the great generals to venture on this First Crusade, having lost in his feud with Bohemond over ownership of Antioch, agreed to lead them. Four thousand more soldiers, led by two other generals, Godfrey of Bouillon and Tancred, joined them on the way, and this was the much-reduced army that would arrive at the gates of Jerusalem.[15]

21. How long did the siege of Jerusalem last?

It was almost biblical—forty days. One problem was that Jerusalem had been retaken by Egyptian Arabs while the Turks were busy with Antioch. The Egyptians were much more accommodating than the Turks and offered several peace plans to the crusaders: safe passage for all unarmed groups to the Holy Land, for example. But the crusaders had not come this far to settle for a peace treaty that they might not trust. They were determined to reclaim the city for Christianity. As Zoe Oldenbourg noted in her history of the Crusades, "The Crusaders did not come to Jerusalem merely to pray and to worship. They were there to fight and to snatch the city from the infidel."[16] In fact, as Jonathan Riley-Smith has pointed out:

One gets the impression of a profound piety, to be seen not only in the willingness to undergo danger and hardship, but also in the large number of visions experienced in the army, in the devotion to certain saints and relics and, above all, in a very typical preoccupation with ritual, which expressed itself in public demonstrations of penitence: indeed in its later stages the crusade resembled a massive, slow-moving liturgical solemnity, culminating in a great penitential procession round the walls of Jerusalem shortly before it fell.[17]

22. How did Jerusalem finally fall to the crusaders?

Prior to the crusader attack, the Christian population of Jerusalem had been expelled, because the Egyptian Arab rulers of the city did not want to repeat the debacle of Antioch whereby the Christian population rose to assist the crusaders once they had attained entry into the city. Several attacks against the walls took place simultaneously. The extent of Jerusalem's walls could both help the defenders by diluting the force of a siege and stretch their resources in resisting a broad assault. This is what happened in the siege of Jerusalem. While crusaders, using huge siege towers, were attacking the walls south and west of Jerusalem, crusaders were also attacking in the north and east. These latter were successful, breaching the northern walls on July 15, 1099, and gaining control of a gate into the city. The crusaders flooded in. Jerusalem was once again, after almost five hundred years of Muslim rule, back in Christian hands. Thomas Madden writes:

> The dream of Urban II had come true. Against all odds, this struggling, fractious, and naïve enterprise had made its way from western Europe to the Middle East and conquered two of the best-defended cities in the western world [Antioch and Jerusalem]. From a modern perspective, one can only marvel at the improbable course of

events that led to these victories. Medieval men and women did not marvel; they merely thanked God.[18]

Pope Urban II, who had begun this most amazing Christian expedition, died two weeks after the conquest of Jerusalem and never heard the news.

23. It is said that, once Jerusalem fell, there was a great massacre of the inhabitants by the crusaders. Did this occur?

The Arab governor was able to purchase his and his court's freedom, but the rest of the population was not so fortunate. With the Christian population previously dismissed, the crusading army found no reason to be discriminating in its passion. Rodney Stark defends this as the rule of the day: when a city resisted a siege, there were no guarantees of mercy. "Had the Muslims surrendered Jerusalem on June 13 when the towers were ready to be rolled against the walls, they would no doubt have been given terms that would have prevented a massacre."[19]

Other historians agree. Even the measured Philip Jenkins urges caution in rushing to judgment: "Though the Western sack of Jerusalem in 1099 is rightly notorious—forty thousand people may have perished—such massacres were far from rare, and Turks were at least as guilty as crusaders."[20] Was this massacre of Jerusalem simply "payback" for previous massacres, or a new and unheard-of atrocity?

The real question seems to be not what the custom of medieval warfare was, but how *Christian* warriors could behave this way. Massacres were commonplace—and the Muslims were not averse to the application of massacre. The massacre of the Christian population at Melitene has already been mentioned (Q. 2). When the Turks destroyed Edessa in 1144 , they killed or enslaved "virtually its entire population, then estimated at 47,000."[21] Again, Saladin massacred the Christian knights, sometimes personally, after their surrender at the Battle of Hattin in 1187. After the Christian knights surrendered at Acre in 1291, they were similarly slaugh-tered. These massacres were certainly comparable to what hap-pened in Jerusalem.[22]

Do these massacres excuse the crusaders? Most modern crit-ics would say no, and the massacre of the populace of Jerusalem seems, by any standards of warfare, to have been extreme. Even Raymond of Toulouse, one of the crusader generals on the scene, condemned the massacre. Accounts of blood going as high the "withers" of horses are no doubt exaggerations of the carnage, but without doubt there was considerable killing of civilians, who in all likelihood had their sympathies with the defenders but were caught in the middle of the combatants.

But it also seems that the massacre, while extensive, was not complete. Crusader generals allowed one group of Arabs to make its way to Damascus and a group of Jews to flee to Ascalon. One recent Jewish historian believes that captured Jews were made to clear the corpses from the city, and letters are extant that begged for funds to ransom captured Jews.[23] That Christian warriors should have risen above such brutality, especially given their high purpose in getting to the Holy Land, is a question that will be long debated.[24]

Whatever the judgment, the crusaders had taken the city, and this brought with it its own jubilation and excess, but a serious fact that needs to be introduced in any assessment of this "massacre" is the news that the port town Ascalon had been taken by an Egyptian army that was known to be marching in support of Jerusalem. This would have lent an urgency to ensuring that the Antioch experience of being besieged and starved was not going to happen again.

24. Did the First Crusade end with the taking of Jerusalem?

Far from it. News of an Egyptian army coming to relieve the besieged Arab forces in Jerusalem was well known to the crusader generals. This news forced them to attack Jerusalem possibly prema-turely, so worried were they about being trapped between the

Jerusalem fortress and the relieving force. This force had now landed at Ascalon, a port on the coast of the Mediterranean, and the crusaders, rather than waiting for it to besiege them in Jerusalem, mounted a surprise attack on the Egyptians and were successful. This action ended the First Crusade. The question now became, "What do we do now?"

25. What *did* the crusaders do after they had taken Jerusalem?

The crusaders tried to establish a Christian empire in the Mideast, one that reached from Jerusalem north to Antioch and east to Edessa. Kings, generals, and governors would take charge of these principalities and fortresses, which would prove to be a source of divisive competition. The governance of conquered lands would prove not only to be a difficult undertaking, because most of the crusaders, having accomplished their task, wanted only to return home to their families, but would also be the final undoing of the crusading mission.[25]

26. At what point did "military orders"— that is, religious orders directly involved in the crusading ideal—begin to form, and what was their function?

Military religious orders are an interesting phenomenon. They formed as soon as Jerusalem was conquered—and for two reasons. One was to continue the crusading spirit and ensure that the military gains would not be lost; the other was to care for the soldiers and pilgrims who were in Jerusalem. The phenomenon of "military orders" grew out of a commitment to religious life, which was widespread at the time, showing itself in the proliferation of religious orders and in their growth. The Cistercians and Carthusians, not to mention the Dominicans and Franciscans, sprang from this enthusiasm. The idea of religious orders committed to the enterprise of the crusade was a variation of that ideal.

In fact, the first such military order, the Knights Hospitaller (or the Order of the Hospital of St. John), was not founded as a military organization at all. Rather, the Hospitallers was begun by monks from the abbey of St. Mary of the Latins in Jerusalem, who founded a hospital in the crusader capital devoted to the care of sick pilgrims.[26] As the number of pilgrims grew in the early twelfth century, the need for the hospital also increased, and the hospital is said to have cared for as many as two thousand people at one time.[27] Seven hundred years before Clara Barton established a nursing corps during the American Civil War, the crusaders had built and staffed, with men and women, the largest hospital in the world. In 1113, this group of medical workers was approved as a separate religious order. They would not be involved in military affairs until twenty years later, when they were given the fortress at Ascalon. Even here, it seems that they hired mercenaries to protect the fortress, while they took care of the hospital.[28] But with time, the number of fortresses given to them began to bring them more into the military sphere without completely eclipsing their commitment to the sick. The Hospitallers eventually had two components: a military and a "hospital" or hospitality component. A member was either a soldier-monk or a hospital-monk, protecting pilgrims on their way to and from the Holy Places or helping them in their distress as doctors and nurses.

The other significant religious order formed to support the Crusades was the Knights Templar (the Order of the Temple of Solomon, begun around 1120). The Knights Templar was begun by Hugh of Payns and eight of his companions, who wanted to devote their lives to the protection of the Holy Land. They were given rooms in a former mosque, which they called the Temple of Solomon. Bernard of Clairvaux promoted this group and gave to it a monastic formation, including the taking of the vows of poverty, chastity, and obedience as well as the donning of a monastic habit: a white robe with a red cross.

A knight in one of these orders also had to commit himself to the defense of the Holy Land by an additional vow. And he had to commit for life. Much of the same vetting that a monk went through to proceed to final vows in a monastery was applied to aspirants to these military orders.

27. Why is there so much mystery about the Knights Templar? Dan Brown's novel *The Da Vinci Code* focused on secrets about Jesus Christ—namely, that he was not God, that he was married to Mary Magdalene, and that this "secret information" had been discovered by the Knights Templar and has been guarded by them through the centuries.

Dan Brown's book is lacking, to say the least, when it comes to historical or biblical accuracy. He pieced things together cleverly, but almost none of it has to do with fact.[29] The Knights Templar built several fortresses along pilgrimage and caravan routes, from which they could both protect pilgrims and tax caravans. In addition, they would fund pilgrims, who could deposit money in a European "temple" (built to resemble the Church of the Holy Sepulchre) and collect it when needed in the Holy Land. This early form of a checking account or "traveler's checks" thus saved the pilgrims from carrying large amounts of cash with them. This innovation eventually made the Templars into one of the most successful banking institutions ever known. When the formal Crusades ended in 1291 with the fall of the port city of Acre, the wealth of the Templars caught the eye of the French king Philip IV, ironically called Philip the Fair. He pursued the Templars ruthlessly because he wanted their land and their money, not because of any secrets they maintained. Pope Clement V, bowing to intense pressure from Philip, formally disbanded them in 1312.

28. Do some of these military orders still exist?

They do, though they do not have a military component. Instead they are worldwide societies that advocate for Christian rights in the Holy Land, provide funds for the maintenance of Christian holy places, and provide scholarships for Christian children to go to school in the Holy Land (widely understood to include the Near East). Two of these orders are known as the Knights of Malta (the descendants of the Knights Hospitallers) and the Knights of the Holy Sepulchre (founded by Godfrey de Bouillon immediately after the conquest of Jerusalem in 1099 and approved by the pope in 1113). These orders have chapters throughout the world.

29. On the whole, were the military orders successful or not?

While the Templars and the Hospitallers were the principal contributors to future crusades, both in terms of finances and manpower, they were eventually defeated. Jerusalem, after all, would not remain in Christian hands. But they sustained the crusades and maintained the high religious purpose behind them. They were, in a sense, the first real *professional* army in Europe since the Roman Empire.

Their downfall was that they were at cross-purposes. Rivalries grew between them about how best to defend the Holy Land—by aggressive raids into unknown country, or by a defensive stance in the various strongholds. One Christian prince, Amalric, repeatedly tried to capture Alexandria. In one assault on the city in 1168, the Templars refused to assist the Hospitallers, who were Amalric's principal military force. These divisions would haunt the Christian occupation of Outremer (which is what the European principalities in the conquered land were called). Also, political leaders (not necessarily from the religious orders themselves) vied for their allegiance in the various intrigues over supreme authority in Jerusalem. The ill-fated assault on Saladin's forces in 1187 was driven by the insecurity of the king, Guy of Lusignan, who had been criticized for failing to attack a Muslim army four years earlier and who now wanted to prove that he was an aggressive and brave leader. He was encouraged in this by Gerald, the head of the Templars, who, for complicated reasons, hated Raymond of Tripoli, who was urging similar (and successful) caution, as had been tried four years before.[30]

Typical of the intrigues in which the military orders were caught is a combination of truces between the Franks and Saladin in 1185, which allowed the latter to consolidate his hold on Syria, and one signed by the Byzantine emperor with Saladin shortly after, thus guaranteeing Saladin his northern flank and allowing him to concentrate his forces on Jerusalem. This lack of unity was ultimately fatal in maintaining Jerusalem as a Christian stronghold.

30. Why was a Second Crusade necessary? Were its goals the same as the First Crusade?

One thing that must be understood is that, despite the eight formal Crusades, relief armies and reinforcements were continuously leaving from European ports to catch up with armies already on the way or in action, to assist at sieges such as at Antioch and at Acre, or to bolster the garrison at Jerusalem. For example, in 1100 largely disorganized relief armies arrived in Asia Minor, with mixed goals and little communication among them.

But major coordinated efforts could be identified as discrete crusades. The Second Crusade was sent to save Antioch and not Jerusalem, which was still safely in the hands of the crusaders. (Remember that the crusaders did not know their crusades as the First or the Second Crusade—that would be left to later historians, much like no one called the Great War "World War I"; that would only come with the Second World War in 1939.) But Antioch was under threat. Edessa, in what might be called the eastern frontier or a buffer state between the Muslims in Iraq (Mosul) and Antioch, had fallen to the Muslim general Zengi in 1144, and Edessa was the gateway to Antioch.[31] It was also the first crusader territory to fall to the Muslims in the forty years of Christian occupation. Imagine the American Civil War: if Atlanta fell, several less-fortified cities in the South would fall in a sort of domino effect: Savannah, Augusta, Charleston, and so forth. When Edessa fell, the entire Norman kingdom was in danger. A Second Crusade was preached to ease the distress of Antioch. It proved to be a disaster. Two western armies, at cross-purposes with each other, not to mention with the Byzantine emperor, who had made a peace treaty with the Turks, were soundly defeated at the old battlefield of Dorylaeum in October 1147. Remnants of the Christian armies limped into Antioch, and the Second Crusade was at an end.

31. Did St. Bernard of Clairvaux preach the Second Crusade? What was his reaction when news of the defeat reached him?

St. Bernard, the great promoter of the austere Cistercian order (they are almost uniformly known to us as Trappists today) who single-handedly founded sixty-six monasteries on his own before his death in 1153, did indeed preach enthusiastically to encourage the formation of the Second Crusade. He saw crusading in rather apocalyptic terms, as God's judgment on his people or his enemies. After the fall of Edessa, Bernard wrote in one letter:

> And now, for our sins, the enemies of the cross have raised blaspheming heads, ravaging with the edge of the sword the land of promise. For they are almost on the point, if there be no one to stop them, of bursting into the very city of the living God, of overturning the sanctuaries of our redemption, of polluting the holy of the spotless Lamb with purple blood.... What are you going to do then, O brave men? What are you going to do, O servants of the cross?[32]

When news of the crushing defeat arrived in Europe, Bernard was heartbroken and sought to make sense of the debacle. He drew an analogy to the ancient Israelites, who were led out of Egypt and into the desert and who struggled because they were not fully committed to the final destination of the Holy Land:

Was there a time in the whole journey when they were not in their hearts returning to Egypt? But if the Jews were vanquished and "perished because of their iniquity" (Psalm 72:19), is it any wonder that those [crusaders] who did likewise suffered a similar fate? Would anyone say that the fate of the former [the Jews] was contrary to God's promise? Neither, therefore, was the fate of the latter [the crusaders]....[33]

Hard words, and probably unfair, given the odds stacked against the crusaders by the opposition of both the Byzantine Empire and Turkish armies. But if one such as Bernard relied on theological motives for warfare, one also needed theological (or biblical) answers for shocking defeat.

32. As I understand it, the aftermath of the Second Crusade made the situation of the crusaders in Jerusalem more critical. How did the Muslim and Christian leaders prepare for the inevitable assault on the Holy City? And how did the Muslim army obtain the surrender of Jerusalem?

A Muslim general (he was actually a Kurd) named al-Malik al-Nasir Salah ed-Din Yusuf, or Saladin, took the initiative. Taking advantage of the bungled crusader incursions into Egypt in 1168 and 1169, the death of the king of Jerusalem (Amalric) in 1174, the Byzantine and Antiochean desire to make peace treaties, thus neutralizing any crusader threat from the north, and Muslim instability in its leadership, Saladin had skillfully united the Egyptian (Fatimid) and Syrian (Abbasid) factions of Islam and played on the crusader leaders' lack of solidarity in how to deal with the threat to Jerusalem. It was a perfect storm.

The Christian leadership had to decide between an aggressive attack on the Muslim army that was amassing north of Jerusalem and a defensive position, staying within the formidable walls of Jerusalem. Initially, Raymond of Tripoli, who had previously made an alliance with Saladin but was now ready to assist with the defense of Jerusalem, convinced the ruler of Jerusalem, Guy of Lusignan, of the wisdom of defense. Guy had previous experience of the success of such strategy but was severely criticized for his "lack of nerve." Gerald, the Templar leader or Master of the Temple, hated Raymond for his alliance with Saladin, during which alliance several Templars were killed, and urged the reluctant Guy to attack. Guy was persuaded and committed the entire crusader army.

Luring this army out into the desert north of Jerusalem, Saladin surrounded and destroyed it at the Battle of Hattin in the summer of 1187. Thomas Madden describes the result:

> The Horns of Hattin marked the greatest defeat in crusading history. Almost all the fighting men in the kingdom were lost, leaving Christian lands defended only by small garrisons in towns and forts. In one disastrous battle, the kingdom of Jerusalem had lost not only its ability to wage war but also its power to defend itself.[34]

The port of Acre surrendered a week after the defeat at Hattin, Ascalon followed suit in September 1187, and Jerusalem in October.

33. Was Saladin the merciful victor he has been portrayed to be?

Saladin cannot be easily portrayed as either merciful or ruthless; he could be both. After the Battle of Hattin he insisted that all the captured knights be beheaded, and in some cases he did the deed personally. When approaching Jerusalem, he threatened to execute the entire Christian population in revenge for the crusader massacre of 1099. He was dissuaded from this by the crusader commander Balian of Ibelin, who was in charge of defending Jerusalem and insisted that he would destroy the city and slay the entire Muslim population of Jerusalem if Saladin did not agree to terms.

Yet, Saladin was known as a man of his word. This is one reason the port cities of Acre and Ascalon surrendered to him without a fight. He was also a pragmatist. Despite the reduced crusader forces within Jerusalem, the siege of Jerusalem took several days until, finally, the walls were breached. But even here, several sorties were repulsed—all the while negotiations about surrender were being carried on between Balian and Saladin. Saladin realized that generous terms would bring about the inevitable victory much sooner, at considerable less loss of life to his own men. Thus the Christian population was granted safe passage to the coast if they purchased their freedom. Many who could not afford the ransom, despite Balian's best efforts to pay for them out of his own funds, were sent into slavery.

Recent attempts to portray Saladin solely as a man of mercy, such as Ridley Scott's movie *The Kingdom of Heaven* (2005), are thus far too simplistic and unhistorical to be taken seriously. Scott, not surprisingly, omits the episode of beheading the knights after Hattin and the selective sending of inhabitants of Jerusalem into slavery.

34. What effect did the loss of Jerusalem to Saladin have on the west?

The Christians of Europe seem to have been surprised and shocked by the surrender of Jerusalem to Saladin. They had grown complacent about the distant war and did not understand the vulnerability of the Latin kingdom in the Near East—not until they heard the unbelievable news. A Third Crusade would be called, and this time the kings of Europe would lead it: Frederick I Barbarossa of Germany, probably the most capable and experienced general of the lot, Richard the Lionheart of England, and Philip II of France—the crusade of the great leaders.[35] Emperors and kings were finally involved. Their reaction was swift. The first to take up arms was a lesser king, William II of Sicily, who dispatched Norman crusaders to Tripoli, just in time to save the city. Frederick's massive army would leave Germany in May 1189. A "Saladin tithe" was levied to pay for the armies, which would prove to be larger than those of the First Crusade.

35. Did the Third Crusade succeed in retaking Jerusalem?

Trouble began for the German crusaders as soon as they reached the Byzantine Empire. The Greek emperor, Isaac II, did not trust Frederick, who bore the title Holy Roman Emperor, long a sticking point with the "Roman Emperor" of the East, and insisted that Frederick surrender the title before proceeding through Byzantine territory. Isaac also signed a secret treaty with Saladin, assuring the latter that he would do everything in his power to impede the progress of these new armies. But Frederick continued on, taking Adrianople and using it as a bargaining chip in negotiating with Isaac, who eventually relented. The secret treaty would be remembered during the next crusade.

Untimely deaths now struck the crusader leadership. William II of Sicily died soon after reinforcing Tripoli, thus stranding his Normans in the port city. Frederick I Barbarossa, who was seventy, died while crossing the River Seleph in Christian Armenia, falling off his horse and into the river, probably the result of a heart attack. This would prove to be a great blow to the venture, as he was the most principled of the generals. His troops were not so principled, and all but a few promptly sailed home.

The French and English armies would go by sea, landing at Tyre, which was still in allied hands, thanks to the audacity of Conrad, who had recently saved Tyre from the brink of capitulating to Saladin. The French arrived first and were immediately plunged into a political struggle between Guy (who had survived the Hattin disaster and still claimed the throne of Jerusalem) and Conrad, who felt that his recent heroics had entitled him to the throne. Another tangled web of crusader intrigue followed as Guy recklessly, though brilliantly, laid siege to Acre. The odds were very much against him, but he could now claim the high ground as a fighter, while Conrad remained in Tyre, consolidating his gains there but coming across as inactive and uninterested in the goal of reclaiming Jerusalem.

Philip II and the French, finding themselves in the awkward position of having to decide between Guy and Conrad, sided with Conrad, backing his claim to be king of Jerusalem if he would join the siege of Acre. Conrad did so, but the siege foundered. Richard the Lionheart, having met resistance in Cyprus from another Greek claimant to the Greek throne, was delayed by having to subdue Cyprus, which he did in 1191. King Guy visited Richard in Cyprus and persuaded him to join the siege and support Guy as the king of Jerusalem. Richard landed ceremoniously, after his navy destroyed a Muslim relief force at sea, and then the crusaders finally obtained the surrender of Acre.

The jealousy of the French king would not permit him to stay, so he sailed home after conceding that Guy would be the king of Jerusalem until his (Guy's) death, after which Conrad would succeed him to the throne. Richard the Lionheart was left to carry on by himself. He slaughtered the Muslim garrison at Acre—some claim as many as 2,500 men—after Saladin did not make good on a first payment of ransom, which included returning the relic of the true cross. He then attempted twice to retake Jerusalem, and both times fell just short of the target. In refusing to take the bait of open battle and almost certain defeat, Richard had learned the lesson of Hattin and saved his army, but he was not able to take Jerusalem, of which Saladin remained in charge. Then, at the news that Philip II was creating mischief by reclaiming English territory in France, Richard returned home in 1192, feeling that he had done his best. Thomas Madden states that the Third Crusade was

> by almost any measure a highly successful expedition:
> Most of Saladin's victories in the wake of Hattin were
> wiped away. The crusader kingdom was healed of its
> divisions, restored to its coastal cities, and secured in a
> peace with its greatest enemy. Although he had failed to

reclaim Jerusalem, Richard had put the Christians of
the Levant back on their feet again.[36]

Unbeknownst to the Europeans, however, it was the last and best
chance that Western Christian armies had of reclaiming Jerusalem.
The following year, 1193, Saladin himself died. But by then the
Third Crusade was a distant memory.

36. Did the failure of the Third Crusade to take Jerusalem crush the crusading spirit in Europe? Would there be a Fourth Crusade?

A new generation of knights wanted to accomplish what
their fathers had been unable to do. A new and young pope in his
thirties, Innocent III, was elected in 1198 and wanted more than
anything else to be known as the pope who succeeded in retaking
the holy places. So a Fourth Crusade was preached.

Richard the Lionheart, who felt that his lands had not been
protected by the papacy in his absence during the Third Crusade,
was not interested and continued to try to reclaim his lands, but he
would die in 1199. Treaties were cobbled together between the
English and the French, and between rival German claimants to
the throne, and a financial deal was made with the Venetians to
transport the armies across the sea.

Despite initial enthusiasm, the Fourth Crusade did not attract
the great numbers of soldiers that its leaders had predicted—only
11,000 of the estimated 35,000 soldiers appeared in Venice, the
marshaling point for the trip to Acre. It also ran out of money.
Hoping to fund the Venetian fleet with payments made by the crusaders themselves, the leaders needed to negotiate with the
Venetian doge in order to meet the shortfall. First on the list was
an agreement to attack a former Venetian colony named Zara,
which was now in the hands of King Emeric of Hungary, a former
crusader himself. The pope had forbidden this, wisely foreseeing
that this would prove a distraction from the supposed purpose of

the crusade and would only be pitting one Christian army against a Christian city.

But the Fourth Crusade had spun out of control, owing to its leaders and their need to fund the remainder of the journey. The next factor to subvert the crusade was the appearance of a Greek prince whose father, Isaac II, had been ousted by his own brother, who had taken the name Alexius III. The young prince, the son of the ousted emperor and the nephew of the usurper, escaped and offered the crusaders a pot of gold: money to finance the voyage and the support of the Byzantine Empire, including troops, in achieving its goals. The crusader leaders and their Venetian sponsors were foolishly convinced by this youngster, who, despite his legitimate claims to the throne, was incapable of making good on his promises.

This created the distraction that Innocent III feared. The crusader leadership had hoped to place the young prince on the throne and be on their way. This did not turn out to be the easy process promised by the heir to the throne, who faced great opposition, and so the crusaders were faced with another winter waiting for promises to be kept. The Greeks overthrew this newly imposed emperor, who was called Alexius IV; opposition grew to the presence of the crusaders, and fighting ensued. The crusaders prevailed in 1204 and established a western kingdom in Constantinople that lasted for about fifty years. Any thought of continuing to Jerusalem was over, and the Fourth Crusade, such as it was, came to an end. Considerable pillaging took place during this occupation, and the relic of the body of St. Mark and the four bronze horses that still stand on St. Mark's Cathedral in Venice were all taken from Constantinople at this time.[37]

37. After the Fourth Crusade, there were two crusades that are not included among the eight organized to retake the Holy Land. Were these two—the Children's Crusade and the Albigensian Crusade—crusades in the strict sense, or were they aberrations or distractions?

These two "crusades" did, in fact, happen, and they need to be discussed. One, the Albigensian Crusade, is definitely more important than the other, but let us begin with the Children's Crusade of 1212. *Something* seems to have happened in the year 1212, as a popular movement made its way from both France and Germany toward the port of Marseilles, with the object of going to Jerusalem to accomplish what the armies could not do. The traditional story is that a shepherd boy in France received a message from Jesus to go on crusade and, when the king of France rejected him, he stirred up a populist movement to support him. Another group from Germany, not be outdone, formed and joined the original child "crusaders." The young group arrived in Marseilles, which was a great slave-trading port. They were put on ships and were promptly sold to Muslims as slaves; some of them were martyred for not converting to Islam.

Although Steven Runciman's history tends to credit this story, which was handed on to us by later chroniclers who described it as a romantic rush of innocent children (*pueri*)—thirty thousand of them by most estimates—there are no contemporary accounts of such a crusade. Most modern scholars question these numbers and the phenomenon, to the point where Tyerman does not even mention it.[38] Jonathan Phillips maintains that some sort of an enthusiastic popular movement occurred that grew out of the frustration with the military, but he too downplays its significance. He maintains that a "few thousand" people had reached the port of Genoa, where

> pragmatic sea captains refused to offer free passage to such a rabble and quickly extinguished the dreams of many of these hopeful, yet utterly naïve, travelers. Some settled in Genoa, others went west to Marseilles where they were also rejected by the seafaring community. The remainder wandered home, no longer welcomed so kindly, but ridiculed for their stupidity.[39]

A recent book, *The Children's Crusade*, is more a historiographical record of what subsequent chroniclers and historians made of the event, but it is surprisingly not helpful in describing what actually happened.[40] However minor the movement seems to have been—an echo of the ill-fated People's Crusade led by Peter the Hermit, but without any organization at all—it was significant enough to catch the eye of the populist pope, Innocent III, who sought to marshal the enthusiasm of common folk in the pursuit of future crusades.

38. You said that the Albigensian Crusade was more important than the Children's Crusade. Can you explain? Was it related, in any way, to the Fourth Crusade?

During the Fourth Crusade, a name turns up that we have not seen before: Simon de Montfort. Simon was in charge of a French force and refused to attack the Christian fortress of Zara because of the pope's threat of excommunication for anyone who did so (see Q. 36). Returning to France, he saw another opportunity for "crusade," but this was an internal affair and had nothing to do with Islam. Southern France was becoming a melting pot due to its proximity to Spain, where Jewish and Muslim peoples influenced the region's social and intellectual life. We see this in the influence of Aristotle's philosophy, which had been preserved by Muslim philosophers and translated by Jewish scholars and then read by Christian theologians such as St. Thomas Aquinas. There were also immigrants lately arrived from the Balkans (where they were known as Bogumils), from which they were being exiled because of their beliefs. They earned the name *Albigensians* because one of their centers of activity was the city of Albi in southwestern France (*gens* in Latin means a citizen; hence, an "Albigens" was a citizen of Albi). Other names, such as "Cathars" or "Manicheans," became synonymous with this movement. They were essentially a revival of the ancient Manichean heresy, of which St. Augustine himself was an adherent for several years. The Manicheans believed that there were two gods: an evil god who created the world and earthly pleasures, and a good god who was a god of light and spirit.

The Albigensians questioned any physical "goods," such as art, music, sport, dancing, and the even more basic physical needs such as reproduction. They opposed marriage because it brought new life into a wicked world. They encouraged suicide. This had repercussions in the world of Christianity because it led to the questioning not only of the whole value of human life, but also, logically, of the value of Christ's becoming man and of the validity of the sacraments, with their physical signs of water, bread and wine, and oil (see QQ. 57–60).

The Albigensian sect began to grow and develop its own church administration and political allies. By 1208 there were four Albigensian bishops in southwestern France—in Toulouse, Carcassonne, Albi, and Agen. Matters came to a crisis when a papal legate, Peter of Castelnau, was murdered while traveling in southern France. The northerners saw this as an attack on their Church, which it was, and decided to eradicate the movement. The pope initially supported this "crusade," granting to these crusaders the same spiritual benefits that were assigned to crusaders going to the Holy Land. He did not realize that it would spiral into a political fight between north and south, between Simon de Montfort and his political enemies, that used the cause of religion as an excuse for bloodshed.

This "crusade" began in 1209 and laid waste to the town of Beziers with such ferocity that other towns capitulated quickly. But Simon now took over and muddied the waters. The northerners were claiming to rid the south of heresy, but several political goals got into the mix, whereby Simon de Montfort revealed his designs of appropriating as much land as possible and becoming the count of Toulouse.

This was close to being a civil war and, as in any civil war, the wounds festered for years. Simon would be killed in 1218 while leading an assault on Toulouse. The fighting in the south continued until the newly crowned King Louis VIII (1223), desirous to go on crusade to the Holy Land, successfully laid siege to Avignon in 1226 and effectively brought the Albigensian Crusade to an end. He died two months later, but negotiations continued until a treaty was signed in Paris in 1229, in which the southern lords recognized the authority of the northern regent, the mother of King Louis IX. Louis was a boy of fifteen at the time and would do much to heal the wounds of this conflict. The pope also tried two important methods of ending the fighting. First, he removed the ecclesiastical incentives to fighting, such as plenary indulgences and the forgiveness of sins and debts, in the hope that the combatants would once again turn their attention to the Holy Land. Second, he introduced the Inquisition as an attempt to legalize the process against the Cathars. This would prove to be, as Thomas Madden points out, "a far more effective tool than large crusading armies."[41] (See QQ. 62–63 for more details on this crusade.) It also clearly delineated the difference between actual heretics and political opponents.

39. The Fifth and Sixth Crusades receive very little attention from historians. What did they accomplish?

Zoe Oldenbourg, in her minor classic *The Crusades*, treats only the first three crusades, as if to comment that the subsequent crusades were not serious attempts to retake the Holy Land, but rather distractions directed toward other goals (Constantinople in the Fourth Crusade), rather half-hearted and ineffective relief expeditions (Fifth and Sixth Crusades), or hopelessly inept sorties that foundered and never got close to Jerusalem (Seventh and Eighth Crusades).[42]

Despite the setbacks of the previous crusades, enthusiasm was hardly on the wane. If the Children's Crusade and the Albigensian Crusade were any indication, the western fighting spirit was still very much alive, but with one very significant difference. While the first crusades saw soldiers dedicated to the final goal and enlisted for the duration, the next crusades saw soldiers signing on for a term, content with having "gone on crusade" without seeing the project to its final goal. Unless they were members of the military orders, crusaders now came and went after short stints, so that their numbers became unpredictable and unreliable. Generals no longer knew how many men they could count on.

Nonetheless, the Fifth Crusade had excellent chances of success and is undeservedly neglected. It began in 1218, as the Albigensian Crusade was near its end. Once again, an approach through Egypt was attempted. The Egyptian Muslims, having surrendered the important city of Damietta, offered the crusaders generous terms, including Jerusalem, but the crusaders, including the Knights Templar and the Hospitallers, advised against such an easy deal, thinking they could have everything: Egypt *and* the Holy Land. Frederick II, the Holy Roman Emperor, kept promising to appear with a great army, but it would take him ten more years before he made an appearance. Another ill-advised crusader raid, this time on Mansurah in Egypt in July 1221 took into account neither the conditions of the desert nor the annual flooding of the Nile and consequently ended in disaster. The terms of surrender demanded by the Muslim generals included the capitulation of Damietta. What had been "on the brink of fantastic success...ended in humiliating failure."[43]

40. Frederick II did arrive, in his own good time, but his crusade (which would be known as the Sixth Crusade) ended in chaos and defeat. How could this happen?

The Sixth Crusade was more of a political fiasco than a military one. There were no battles. No attack on Jerusalem was ever carried out. Instead, the crusaders watched as Frederick II, the German Holy Roman Emperor, negotiated a truce with the Muslim occupiers of Jerusalem, vowing not to reinforce the city, not to help in any fight against Muslims, and so forth. The deal he struck was shameless. He had been excommunicated by the pope and shunned by the military orders as a result. He had promised ten years earlier to come to the help of the crusaders and only now appeared to claim a crown. Frederick wanted to be the king of Jerusalem, and he seemed not to care what this title meant for the crusading effort. He was crowned in the Church of the Holy Sepulchre and quickly departed for home, being pelted with garbage as he made his way through the streets of Acre to his waiting ships.

41. What was the lure of Egypt? Why did one crusading general after another want to neutralize Egypt before taking Jerusalem?

Egypt was seen as the soft underbelly of the crusader states in the Levant. As we have seen, Amalric, while king of Jerusalem, seemed fixated on taking Egypt, sending troops to reduce the port of Damietta and besiege Alexandria. Richard the Lionheart wanted to take Egypt before attacking Jerusalem. The Fourth Crusade, before it got sidetracked into attacking Constantinople, was headed toward Egypt. The Fifth Crusade wanted to take Damietta, which it did, and was lured farther south to Mansurah (with Cairo as its ultimate destination), where it perished.

Egypt was a Muslim stronghold, a source of money and soldiers for Muslim armies, a continual irritant to crusaders along the Levant coast. Saladin needed to unite with the Egyptians before assaulting Jerusalem. So it was thought that the neutralizing of Egypt was a key to a permanent success in the Holy Land. The fact that the Muslim generals always demanded the return of Damietta in all surrender negotiations shows the importance of the port for them as well. It was a lure that would continue to the very last crusades, as Louis IX of France sought to begin his crusades by conquering Egypt.

42. King Louis IX of France thought he knew the way to end the impasse, not only of the bitter feelings surrounding the northern incursion into Albigensian territory in his own country, but also of reconquering Jerusalem. What was *his* plan?

King Louis IX, who would later be known to us as St. Louis, had an original idea. He had just experienced a civil war in his country, the Albigensian Crusade (see Q. 38), and certainly the bitter results and resentments that followed it. Even though he was only a boy when the peace between the two factions was finally agreed on, Louis wanted to unify his country. He thought that he could encourage the northern and southern lords of his divided country to go on crusade in a united effort and thereby bring his divided country together. A common enemy can be a compelling source of unity.

43. Did Louis IX's attempt to unify his country work?

As a matter of fact, it did, even though the ultimate object, the conquest of Jerusalem, would be denied him. Lands were granted to southern lords for agreeing to go on pilgrimage, which served to restore lands and titles that had been taken from them during the Albigensian Crusade. The result of Louis IX's efforts was the unification of his country, which is now known to us as France. When he began his enterprise, this "country" was seriously divided—especially in religion and language—and his efforts brought both sections together.[44]

44. Did Louis IX propose a plan of attack that was different from previous Crusades?

Like so many military leaders before him, Louis thought that the best approach to Jerusalem was through Egypt. Much time and energy had been lost in past crusades by slogging through Asia Minor and dealing with the troublesome Byzantines. Landing in Acre would be easy, but it would not take care of the worrisome Egyptians to the south. It seemed that victory had been in the grasp of the Fifth Crusade and that a similar mission, if better organized and more capably led, could succeed.

This crusade, known as the Seventh Crusade, started well but ran aground fairly soon. Once again, the port of Damietta was the initial target and was taken easily. Too easily, in fact. What took the armies of the Fifth Crusade eighteen months to accomplish was managed by Louis almost overnight. Louis wanted to avoid the mistakes of the Fifth Crusade, but he found himself repeating them. Instead of securing Damietta and moving north, he felt the lure of capturing Egypt once and for all. The ease with which he took Damietta misled him into thinking that a similar easy victory awaited him to the south. It was not to be so. The town of Mansurah would once again resist the crusaders' best efforts. Louis surrendered and was held for ransom; eventually he was released and journeyed to the Holy Land to fund the improvement of defenses along the coastal garrisons.

45. Louis IX would not let go of his dream to take back Jerusalem, so he called for another expedition, the Eighth Crusade. What was the purpose of this crusade? Did it fare any better than the rest?

Louis's high purpose was always to restore Jerusalem to Christianity. But he was getting old and was running out of time. Once again, contrary to good advice, he organized this last crusade and set sail in July 1270. Much to everyone's surprise, he decided to attack the relatively minor stronghold of Tunis, thinking he was removing an Egyptian ally from the equation. Almost nothing went right in this expedition: allies failed to appear on time, mid-summer conditions were appalling, and many soldiers, including Louis's son, died of disease. Louis himself followed suit, dying of dysentery in 1270—a martyr to the cause of trying to reclaim the Holy Land (as he would have liked to imagine), with the words "O Jerusalem! O Jerusalem!" on his lips as he expired.

46. The Eighth Crusade would prove to be the last formal crusade by an organized western military force to recover Jerusalem. What happened after Louis's failure?

The military orders hung on for a time, manning the various fortresses along the pilgrim route. But their fortresses became isolated and they could not support one another. These fell one by one, including the formidable castle Crac du Chevaliers, until only the port city of Acre was left. It fell to a Muslim attack in 1291. All of the knights were executed.[45]

47. Were other crusades organized to retake the Holy Land, even after the eight formal crusades had ended?

The fighting continued, but the battles could hardly be called crusades in the same sense as those of 1096–1270. They became defensive actions aimed at preventing the Turks from making even more incursions into the Balkan Peninsula or Italy. One battle, Nicopolis, took place in 1396 along the Danube in what is now Bulgaria and was a disaster for western allied armies. Once again, they did not have a central command and fought the Muslims in a totally disorganized and undisciplined way, with generals vying for notoriety and fame rather than victory.[46]

Constantinople itself would fall to the Turks in 1453. Constantinople had relied on technology to defend itself ever since the 700s, when it repelled a serious Arab assault by relying on its massive walls and "Greek fire," a medieval form of the modern flame thrower. But technology would outpace the Greeks. In the mid-1400s, the Turks enlisted the help of a European expert in the new art of demolition by cannon fire to try to breach the walls of Constantinople. The Byzantines were caught between a rock and a hard place. They wanted to resist Turkish invasions and occupation of their empire, but they also were suspicious that the westerners were no better and would similarly occupy their land. However, their preoccupation with maintaining their kingdom as it had been for centuries would cost them everything.

48. All of that being said, the combination of the victories at Nicopolis and Constantinople opened Eastern Europe to the Turks. What prevented them from taking advantage of their newfound gains?

Two things. One is that they seemed to have been distracted by Italy, which was undergoing a Renaissance. The Turks attacked Otranto, on the boot of Italy, in 1481, sawing the mayor and the elderly archbishop in half. This attack managed finally to galvanize the Italian city-states, which put together an armada led by a cardinal (which gives an insight into the Church at the time). This armada recaptured the city and restored the peninsula to the Italians.

The second problem faced by the Turks was the figure of the Holy Roman Emperor, Charles V, the king of Spain. Charles set aside his quarrels with German princes who were using a troublesome monk named Martin Luther to focus grievances against Charles's rule and the Church in order to expend considerable effort in stemming the Turkish inroads into Europe. Luther defied the pope in 1517. Belgrade fell to the Turks in 1521, and in 1529 the Turks laid siege to Vienna, which narrowly escaped capture. These events are not unrelated, and some historians claim that Protestantism succeeded only because of the threat of the Turks to the Holy Roman Empire in the mid-1500s.[47] It is probably more complicated than that, because Lutheranism had a popular appeal of its own, but it is true that the Holy Roman Emperor had to make compromises with the Lutherans in order to keep down the threat of the Turks. Such distractions allowed Lutheranism to continue and spread. Had there been no Turkish threat to his empire, Charles could have made the Lutheran princes the object of his military might and things may have gone differently for Lutheranism specifically and for Protestantism generally. Also, any idea of crusade in the future seemed impossible, given the divisions within Christian Europe. Only a pope seemed capable of calling a crusade, and half of Europe was paying no attention to the pope.

The next major battle was the naval battle of Lepanto, off the coast of Asia Minor, in 1571. It was decisive in many ways. The Turks never tried seriously to invade Europe for another hundred years and lost any advantage they might have by sea. But also the story was put out that the pope, a Dominican named Pius V, was praying the Rosary on the day of the battle (October 7) and had a vision that the Christian navies had been victorious. He would not hear news of the battle for another week and, after he did, he proclaimed October 7 to be the feast of Our Lady of Victory. Later this was toned down to be the feast of Our Lady of the Rosary, long a cherished devotion of the Dominican Order and a feast still celebrated to this day.

One last significant battle waited to be fought. Turks moved up the Adriatic coast and laid siege to Vienna again in 1683. This was a serious threat to all of Europe. A Polish army led by Jan Sobieski came south to defeat the Muslims decisively.[48] Active fighting between Christians and Muslims would end with this battle.

49. You haven't mentioned the Reconquista, which was the Christian reconquest of Muslim Spain. How was this connected to the Crusades going off to the Holy Land and even the Albigensian Crusade?

The Reconquista tried to do on a national level (Spain and Portugal) what the Crusades were trying to do on an international level. Beginning in 1066, the Spanish, through a series of military surges, attempted to retake the Iberian peninsula from the Muslims. They would finally succeed in 1492 with the fall of Granada. Just as in the aftermath of the Albigensian Crusade the Inquisition was instituted as a means of consolidating legally the gains made by fighting but also of replacing the fighting with a legal process, so too the Reconquista was followed closely by the Spanish Inquisition (which actually began ten years before the fall of Granada), which tried to finalize, legally and judicially, what the Reconquista had accomplished militarily. This allowed the conquerors of Granada, the *conquistadores*, to go to the New World. I will discuss both of these inquisitions in much more detail in the second half of this book.

50. Why did the Crusades to the Holy Land ultimately fail?

A reading of the accounts of the eight Crusades leads one to conclude that several factors contributed to the western failure to gain permanent control of the Holy Land.

1. A lack of centralized command. Generals went off with their personal armies, with little sense of coordinated attack or defense. Jealousies fueled personal feuds between rival generals. These generals often refused to cooperate with one another and sometimes undermined the efforts of others. King Philip of France would not fight with Richard the Lionheart after Acre had been taken in the Third Crusade. Conrad would initially not fight with King Guy in his siege of Acre. Everyone seemed to be returning to Europe in a huff over some slight.

2. Generals could not divorce themselves from personal conquest. When Bohemond defeated the Turkish general Kerbogha at Antioch, he felt that Antioch was his by right. Allied commanders seemed anxious to establish their own kingdoms in Tarsus (at which they were unsuccessful) and Edessa. When Conrad saved the port of Tyre, he felt that the title of "king of Jerusalem" was his by right. The Byzantine emperor did not want to assist Frederick I Barbarossa because he bore the title "Holy Roman Emperor."

3. Military units seemed unable to continue without their chosen leader. When Barbarossa died during the Third Crusade, most of his army went home. When William II of Sicily died after saving Tripoli, his Normans seemed incapable of moving on. The one exception to this was after the fall of Antioch, when none of the leaders was anxious

to move on toward Jerusalem, and the common soldier propelled the final drive.

4. The relationship between the Byzantine emperors and the western crusaders was poisonous. The distrust between the two ran deep, their different goals frequently conflicted, and suspicions of each other's intentions prevented serious and reliable cooperation.

5. Finally, I think, the distances proved too great. It is difficult to sustain interest in a war being waged thousands of miles away, where no local or national interests seemed at stake. What is possibly most remarkable about the eight Crusades is that they occurred over *such* a long period of time.

Ironically, the same conditions applied to Muslim Spain, but in reverse. Muslim leadership was divided without central command; they were divided about goals and about what kind of Islam was to be imposed. Treaties were frequently made between Muslim and Christian generals in order to eradicate some threat from a Muslim sect or leader. Radical Muslims from North Africa sought to impose their law on Spain, much to the horror of Muslims already occupying Spain. This lack of unity would prove the undoing of the Muslim occupation of Spain and Portugal.

51. Were the Crusades nothing more than "a long act of intolerance in the name of God," or a medieval manifestation of Islamophobia?

The Crusades were not initiated by westerners out of their intolerance for Islam;[49] they began because of a combination of anger at Turkish intolerance of native Christian populations in the Near East and the intimidation of Christian pilgrims to the Holy Places. Even Egyptian caretakers of Jerusalem had had a respect for the Christian Holy Places and allowed Christians to visit and venerate them. So to identify this collective anger, experienced by the crusaders, as Islamophobia is misdirected. The term *Islamophobia* connotes a fear of something that is not present, a fear that is irrational, and possibly a fear that is encouraged for political ends, much like the fear of the Jews was encouraged by the Nazis before World War II.

But such was not the case with the Christian Crusades to the Holy Land. There was a genuine fear that Islam threatened the existence of Christianity, not only in the Holy Land, but in Spain as well, not to mention the Christianity of the Byzantine world and the very existence of Byzantium and potentially of Christian Europe. These threats were not imagined; they were actually being carried out. Pope Urban II's clarion call at the Council of Clermont was not propaganda or hype, though there may have been a bit of both in his speech; it was a wake-up call. Urban exhorted Europe to put aside its internal feuding and come to the aid of its Christian brethren living in the East:

> For the Turks, a Persian people, have attacked them, as many of you already know, and have advanced as far into Roman territory as that part of the Mediterranean which is called the Arm of St. George [Bulgaria]. They have seized more and more of the lands of the Christians, have already defeated them in seven times as many battles, killed or captured many people, have destroyed churches, and have devastated the Kingdom of God. If you allow them to continue much longer they will conquer God's faithful people much more extensively.[50]

The accusations of Islamophobia leveled during our own time are also frequently misplaced. While there are people in the West who want, without justification, to suspect any Muslim of terrorism, the fact is that the Christian West has been tolerant of Islam, allowing its adherents to build mosques and worship publicly and be part of the social fabric anywhere they choose. In Arab countries, such toleration of Christians increasingly is not seen.[51] A recent article in *Newsweek* ("The Global War on Christians in the Muslim World" by Ayaan Hirsi Ali, February 6, 2012) documents attacks on Christian enclaves and churches in Sudan and Nigeria, where Boko Haram, the Muslim extremist group, killed at least 510 Christians in 2011, burned down or destroyed more than 350 churches in ten northern Nigerian states—attacking one Catholic church on Christmas day and killing forty-two Catholics—and killed another fifty-four Christians in January 2012 alone.[52] This is not to mention the intimidation of Christians in Iraq, Egypt, Lebanon, Indonesia, and other parts of the Muslim world, where Christians have to fight, sometimes physically, to survive. Such threats are not imagined; they are real.[53]

To label the crusader fear of radical Islam in the Middle Ages as Islamophobia when even other Muslims (Egyptian Arabs and Spanish Muslims) were as afraid of their radical coreligionists as were the westerners is to trivialize a serious threat that still exists today. To categorize all Muslims as terrorists is obviously wrong, but to dismiss fear of radical Islam as Islamophobia is also obviously missing the lessons of history.

The Inquisition

52. How can you make the claim that the Inquisition and the Crusades are related?

I have already shown that there seems to be a strong connection between the crusading movement and the phenomenon of the Inquisition (Q. 38). This connection is not merely chronological or accidental—as if the Inquisition simply happened to follow the crusading movements. Although inquisitions clearly followed on the heels of these military operations, and especially the Albigensian Crusade and the Reconquista, the movements seem to be intimately related. They attempted to accomplish, to a great extent, the same goals: a political and spiritual unity either within France or Spanish territory. In the case of the Albigensian Crusade and the ensuing Medieval Inquisition, this entailed the unification of France; in the case of the Reconquista, the Spanish Inquisition entailed the unification of Spain and its territories (especially in the New World). This did not apply to the eight formal Crusades that were organized in support of the Holy Land, because there was never time for an enforcing agency to follow up on the work of conquest. The warriors of the Holy Land were far more occupied with survival.

But the Inquisition tried to do both more and less than the violence it sought to replace: more in the sense that it introduced a legal process by which a wide range of heresies would be addressed, and less in that it narrowed its energies to theological issues. It did not always succeed in these two aims, and it could be used (either by politicians or churchmen) to spread its theological reach too far—such as when Ignatius Loyola and Teresa of Avila were both threatened by ecclesiastical censure—or to blur the lines between theological error and political opposition, as when Joan of Arc was accused of witchcraft.

Despite the abuses, which are fully treated in this book later on, the institution of the Inquisition can be seen as a replacement for the military action it followed. That it succeeded in this and was a noble and civilizing force in pursuing truth, and was not a prostitution of Church power and an obvious attempt to silence dissent, or something in between, is something I hope to show in the following pages.

53. It would seem that comparing the Medieval Inquisition with the Spanish Inquisition is quite ambitious, since they occurred hundreds of years apart and began in very different circumstances. How do they compare?

You are quite correct in noticing the differences, and critics of the Inquisition have made a serious mistake in confusing the two. Edward Peters is characteristically astute in distinguishing them as he does.[1] Recent authors have focused solely on the Spanish Inquisition and its offshoots.[2] But others, I think to good effect, have treated both under one cover.[3] I believe it is instructive to do so here.

The Medieval Inquisition began toward the end of the twelfth century and had as its subjects both Albigensian and Waldensian heretics (see QQ. 54–60). The formation of the Medieval Inquisition developed quickly from a diocesan juridical process under the direction of the local bishop to a juridical process controlled by the pope. The Spanish Inquisition, however, was aimed initially at Jewish and Muslim converts to Christianity who could be accused of secretly continuing Jewish or Muslim rituals. This Inquisition was initiated and driven by the Spanish monarchs Ferdinand and Isabella, considerably outside the jurisdiction of the pope, and could be considered a much more "national" phenomenon. (Similar inquisitions would occur in Portugal, Venice, Rome, Naples, and other places.) The methods of both inquisitions were very similar, and the involvement of the friars (mostly Dominicans) was also a shared feature. But eventually the Spanish Inquisition turned its attention to Catholic conformity, so much so that most of its trials for "heresy" involved errors of Catholic thinking or practice. The fact that both Inquisitions followed on military action, and replaced it, cannot be denied.

54. Other than the desire to replace military action with a legal process, what other factors contributed to the rise of the Inquisition in Europe in the twelfth and thirteenth centuries?

Europe was experiencing a new energy, one that involved the growth of cities and universities, the building of cathedrals, and the development of art, music, and literature. Much of this energy was religious and was fueled by the renewal of religious life and the revival of theological studies based on the rediscovery of Aristotle's philosophy.

The Benedictine order, founded by St. Benedict in the sixth century, saw an amazing growth beginning with the foundation of the abbey of Cluny in 909. Soon daughter houses were springing up throughout Europe. Variations on the Rule of St. Benedict also appeared. The Carthusians were founded by St. Bruno in 1084 in an attempt to revive the Eastern or Egyptian model of religious life with its emphasis on solitude. Shortly after, the Cistercians, with their emphasis on silence and austerity, were founded in 1098 with St. Bernard as its most famous son. When he died in 1153 there were already 343 Cistercian abbeys and, by 1300, that number would be more than doubled. St. Norbert founded the Premon-stratensians in the southern French town of Prémontré in 1119. A revolution in religious life would appear with the founding of the friars, the Dominicans and Franciscans, which were formally approved by the pope in 1216 and 1223, respectively. This new form of religious life introduced democracy at every level of their governments and allowed for mobility, which would prove to be a critical counter to the heresies of the age.

When such energy exists, shoots sprout in all directions, some of them perfectly orthodox, but others "on the edge" or "over the edge." It was not immediately clear which groups fell into which categories. Were Norbert's and Francis's followers simply alterna-tive expressions of the Waldensian heresy? Some churchmen thought so, and they urged both men to try out their religious energy in already established orders. In neither case did this work. Norbert was finally allowed to begin his order on an experimen-tal basis, and Pope Innocent III had the wisdom to permit Francis to proceed, despite considerable opposition from his curia, with the proviso that Francis be ordained to the diaconate.

While it welcomed such enthusiasm and innovation, the Church found a need to monitor their directions, ensuring that orthodoxy of doctrine was maintained and that discipline was not compromised by an abandonment of rules and law. Hence, there was a need to oversee the new developments and keep in check those movements that seemed capable of doing more harm than good.

55. Which religious movements seemed capable of "doing more harm than good" or appeared to be going astray?

It is important to remember that the original lines between orthodoxy and heresy could sometimes be blurry and only later would be clarified. It would be helpful here to divide the "prob-lem movements" into two different categories: Waldenses and Albigensians. There would be later movements, such as those led by John Wycliffe and Jan Hus in the fourteenth and fifteenth cen-turies, but they were considerably different from the groups of the thirteenth century in that their issues were much more germane to the Reformation; Wycliffe's demands were nearly identical to Luther's, even though he predated Luther by 150 years. And the Inquisition did not deal with these latter groups with the same intensity with which it focused on Waldenses and Albigensians. Wycliffe and Hus were condemned by papal and conciliar deci-sions rather than by the methods of the Inquisition.

56. Many authors are of the opinion that the Waldenses were condemned more for political reasons than for theological ones, that they were a threat more to the organization or political fabric of the Church than to its doctrinal core. How valid is that observation?

The name *Waldenses* derives from a certain Peter Waldo or Valdes who, about the year 1179, dedicated himself completely to the ministry of evangelical (gospel-based) preaching. He and his followers, centered in southeastern France near Lyons, believed that the official Church had lost its grounding in scripture and was becoming lax or distant, unintelligent (especially in its parochial clergy), and overly elitist and bureaucratic. They saw that this affected the average believer in a detrimental way and wanted to get more serious about religion, especially at the lay level. Why should a genuinely Christian life infused with a deep spirituality be limited to someone who joined a religious order or was ordained? Why cannot the fruits of the scriptures be made available to the "person in the pew"?

This was compelling stuff and attracted a considerable following. In fact, Norbert's and Francis's religious orders were direct results of this movement. Live poorly, follow the message of the gospel, preach a message of personal moral reform, and avoid the intrigues of a hierarchical and politically charged Church. Herbert Grundmann, in his trend-setting history of religious movements in the Middle Ages, thought that movements such as the Waldenses were not heretical movements at all, in the strict sense of being theological deviations from Christian orthodoxy, but were merely challenges to the authority of the Church.[4] More recently, Alister McGrath agrees and states that the Inquisition, in including the Waldenses under its designation as heresy, "represents a significant move away from patristic attempts to encapsulate the essence of heresy, which focused on the threat it posed to the Christian faith as a whole—not to Christian individuals or institutions."[5]

There is a flaw in this separation of faith and institution. The Church, from its inception, has always recognized that the content of the faith is overseen and guaranteed by the institution, which is itself an entity founded by Christ. There is a reason for this. To separate the content of faith from the community of believers and their leaders is to wade into dangerous waters. St. Paul spent his entire missionary life trying to ensure that this did not happen. It is not enough to say that the Waldenses merely threatened the Church's monopoly on the interpretation of scripture; as time went on their interpretations came close to questioning important tenets of faith: the effectiveness of sacraments, the institution of the priesthood (and episcopacy), the authority of the Church to define and safeguard the content of the faith. It led eventually to Wycliffe's claim that the Mass was not to be found in scripture and that the only certain rule of faith was to be found in scripture, which everyone must interpret for himself, an idea that McGrath describes as the "democratization of biblical interpretation."[6]

The Church authorities in the twelfth century saw where the Waldenses were headed and tried to direct them to safer ground, as they did with Norbert and Francis, but they did not always meet with similar agreement.[7]

57. The other group mentioned as possibly being "over the edge" was the Albigensians. Who were they and how did they get their name?

The name derives from the town of Albi, which became the hub of Cathar activity (see Q. 59), much like Münster in Germany drew Anabaptists in the sixteenth century, and Strasbourg and Geneva attracted Protestants during the early Reformation. One might compare the phenomenon (I hope without being facetious) to hippies coming to San Francisco in the 1960s. It was where you met your confreres, shared common ideas, could sing in public, dress as you like, feel safe, and so forth. An *Albigens* was, according to the Latin, a citizen of Albi.

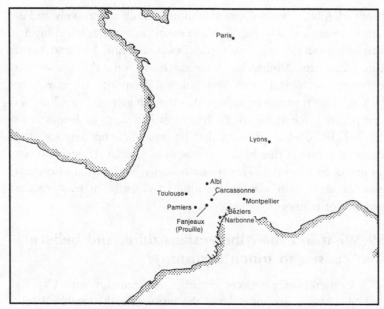

MAP 2: THE ALBIGENSIAN CRUSADE AND THE MEDIEVAL INQUISITION

58. The area influenced by Albigensians seems to be fairly insignificant. Why did Albigensianism attract the attention that it did from both the northern French nobility and the Church?

The heartland of Albigensianism was bounded by a line connecting Toulouse (the major city in the area), Albi, Carcassonne, and Foix, with the highest concentration of Albigensians lying along the line from Toulouse to Carcassonne (see map 2). Nearly all of the nobility in this area of southern France, including the towns of Laurac, Montreal, and Fanjeaux, had either become Albigensians or were aligned with them. The nobles were not necessarily drawn to Albigensianism for theological reasons, but because it provided the best political focal point for opposition to both the Church and the northern nobility (and eventually the king) in feuds over property, wealth, privilege, and power. As long as these feuds remained peaceful, Albigensianism spread, although more aggressively and in a more organized way than Waldensianism: there were four Albigensian bishops in this area—in Toulouse, Carcassonne, Albi, and Agen. But when the Albigensian Crusade broke out, the distinction between theological error and political animosity became very blurred. This is precisely what makes the Albigensian "problem" so complicated. When Simon de Montfort laid siege to Toulouse in 1217–1218 (on the grounds that he was pursuing heretics), the count of Toulouse (the besieged) was, in fact, *not* an Albigensian but an orthodox Christian. This is one reason why the Inquisition was established: to stop exactly this kind of violence, at least on the grounds of religion.

59. What did the Albigensians think and believe that caused so much acrimony?

Contemporary writers identified Albigensians with Cathars and Manicheans and often used the terms interchangeably. While this identification may be technically imprecise, there are enough similarities among the three groups to see why they would have been confused. Manicheism has the longest pedigree and goes back at least to the third century, when it attempted to solve the problem of the existence of evil in the world by positing two equal forces in the world: one for good and one for evil. The evil force was a creating force, or god, and brought into the world things that were imperfect, limited, changeable, and mortal. The good force was perfect and called people to transcend their mortal existence.[8]

Albigensianism was, to an extent, a revival of this idea, and was possibly spurred on by the arrival in southern France of Bogumils (or Cathars), who were being expelled from the Balkans by the Byzantine emperor. Thus Albigensianism became a curious blend of Manichean and Christian elements—especially institutional elements such as bishops and quasi-sacramental rituals.

A hallmark of Albigensianism was a fear of the physical. The notion of a god or force creating evil led to a suspicion of created things, which had moral, societal, and theological implications.

Physical pleasures seemed almost necessarily to lead to excess and frustration. Dance, music, art, or sport became suspect. Parish fairs and festivals, which might include drinking and gambling, singing and dancing, were denounced. Celibacy was encouraged, not merely as a discipline, but as a positive act of preventing new life from coming into the world. The notion of God becoming a human being was unthinkable, and sacraments, with their reliance on physical symbols, were rejected. The liturgy, with its use of candles, incense, vestments, art, and music, was similarly disparaged. The Albigensians replaced Christian baptism with a substitute rite, called the *consolamentum*, that was a baptism of the Spirit and did not involve the use of water.

60. Why did the religious approach of the Albigensians become as popular as it did?

The extent of the popularity of Albigensianism is a subject for debate, as is the popularity of the later Wycliffites or Lollards.[9] The best research suggests that they were a minority, but a significant one. Albigensians certainly existed in such numbers as to worry the northern lords and the Church. While St. Dominic was traveling through Albigensian country on his way from Spain to Rome in 1203, he noticed the extent and attractiveness of Albigensianism and the commitment of its adherents to such a degree that he devoted the rest of his life to addressing its issues (see Q. 64).

It is difficult to account for the attractiveness of seemingly strict and rigid movements within religions. As one Dominican priest pointed out, "They are the grim bearers of the glad tidings." Without going into a history of religion, it seems that most mainline religions, whether Christian or not, have within them a certain faction that demands stricter morality and a more fundamental understanding of their holy writings. We see this in the early Church with Montanism, Donatism, and Pelagianism. We see it in religious life, when reform movements (such as the Cistercians) call for stricter observance of the rule of their founders. Nearly all religious orders would see reform movements within them: the Franciscans would see the formation of the Observant Franciscans and then the Capuchins, the Dominicans the rise of the preacher Savonarola, the Carmelites the formation of the reformed (Discalced) Carmelites led by Teresa of Avila and John of the Cross. It will appear in the Protestant world as Calvinism and Puritanism and, in the Catholic lay world, as Jansenism.[10] And we see it in Albigensianism. These movements tend to go in cycles in response to laxity or moral decay within the main body.

It is fair to say that the religious energy of the Middle Ages gave birth to several movements—the Cistercian and Carthusian orders, the orders founded by Norbert and Francis, Waldensianism and Albigensianism—that expected a *moral rigor* (as opposed to doctrinal precision) from their believers and had them respond to the challenge of the gospel to put its imperatives into effect. Albigensianism attracted followers because it offered a coherent program that attempted to merge a worldview of good versus evil with a practical and, in some ways, a simple human response: avoid the temptations of the flesh. It attracted adherents precisely because it was demanding, much like Calvinism's principal appeal was moral rigor. People wanted to be better, and Albigensianism offered them a way to do it. Because its moral program (the renunciation of marriage and the eating of eggs, meat, and milk) was so severe, only a small core of truly committed Albigensians, known as "perfects," was admitted. The historian Riley-Smith estimates that there were only about one thousand perfects in the region of southern France between 1200 and 1209, although about 35 percent of them were nobility.[11]

61. How did society and the Church respond to these movements?

There was a three-pronged response. The first, as we have seen (QQ. 1, 38), was an armed crusade called the Albigensian Crusade, a crusade within the Crusades that were still going off to the Holy Land; the second was through education and especially preaching; and the third was by legislation and prosecution. The combination of these three reactions, over the course of one hundred years, almost eliminated Albigensianism by the year 1330.

62. Why was armed crusade used in an attempt to eradicate Albigensianism? Was it successful?

Because the armed assault on Albigensian strongholds, known as the Albigensian Crusade, led directly to the institution of the inquisition trials for heresy, it is good to begin here. The northern lords were upset with what was happening in the south, both from a political and a religious point of view. Southern nobility were becoming more independent and assertive in their desire for land and privilege, and the religious trend of Albigensianism, which they were seizing upon as an additional weapon, was unsettling. There seemed to be no way to address these issues legally, so the only alternative was violence.

The idea of how to correct these "differences" was brutal and undiscriminating. The first military attack on Albigensians was organized in 1181 by Abbot Henry of Clairvaux, who instigated a successful attack on the castle of Lavaur, home to Roger Trenceval II, who had imprisoned the orthodox Christian bishop of Albi.[12]

But it was not until 1208, when the papal delegate Peter of Castelnau, who was sent by the pope precisely to ameliorate the difficulties, was murdered, that the first military *campaign* was requested by Pope Innocent III and was launched. The northerners hardly needed to be asked. Arnold Aimery, the northern general, captured Beziers and boasted that he had killed fifteen thousand people, which was certainly an exaggeration.[13]

Carcassonne was next in Arnold's path and was besieged by as many as twenty thousand soldiers. The crusaders had a list of wanted people, and they demanded that those individuals be handed over to them. If the town refused, the crusaders killed anyone they could find. This served to intimidate other towns in the area and they were quickly brought to heel: Fanjeaux, Montreal, Mirepoix, Limoux, Pamiers, Castres, Lombers, and Albi all surrendered without fighting. The Albigensian faithful went underground, traveling by night, meeting in secret, even exempting adherents from their own rules (against taking an oath, for example, or eating meat) if it might help them avoid capture.

At this point Simon de Montfort became head of the army. He continued the brutality. Under his leadership, 140 Cathars were burned to death at one time in the town of Minèrve, and between three and four hundred were killed after a second capture of Lavaur. Simon, who wanted to become the count of Toulouse, laid siege to the city but died in the attempt.

In 1226, King Louis VIII, tired of the continued fighting in the south and wanting to go on crusade to the Holy Land, invaded the south with his army, successfully laying siege to Avignon and effectively bringing the Albigensian Crusade to an end. The southerners trusted him far more than they did the northern nobility. In 1229, the Treaty of Paris was signed by the southern nobles and the crown. Still, considerable mending needed to be done. The king's son, who would become Louis IX (and then St. Louis), was only fifteen years old when the Peace of Paris was signed. In his own desire to go on crusade, he offered the southern nobility concessions of land and titles for their cooperation in joining him. He would fail in his two attempts to capture Jerusalem, but in the process of fighting, he successfully united both the northern and southern parts of France into the country we recognize today.

63. Did the Albigensian Crusade succeed in ridding the south of France of heresy?

No, and thus other means were brought to bear. The pope had seen the political direction taken by Simon de Montfort and began to withdraw privileges previously granted to Albigensian crusaders, such as protection of land while on campaign and plenary indulgences, desiring instead that they go to the Holy Land.

Crusading in southern France was also a cyclical affair, something that occurred only in the summer. Soldiers enlisted for forty days. During this time the generals had to subdue the towns and land they were seeking as efficiently as possible. This explains why the campaigns were so brutal. It was also difficult to hold onto the captured property during the fall and winter, when the soldiers went home to harvest their crops. Something more permanent was needed. The solution was the combination of preaching and inquisition.

64. Why did St. Dominic arrive at *preaching* as a way of combating what he saw as a distorted view of life in Albigensianism?

Dominic witnessed the power of lay preaching as he was passing through Languedoc in 1203, the commitment of the Albigensians to their way of life, the compelling witness of poverty, and the simplicity of the Albigensian message. The answer, he thought, was in imitating the Albigensians in their lifestyle: by embracing mobility, poverty, and emphasis on the gospel. Albigensians preached the Gospel according to John, which can be seen as more "otherworldly" and spiritual than the more earthy Synoptic Gospels. John does not begin with the birth of Christ, but with the "light coming into the world." Jesus was the "Word." So Dominic preached the Gospel according to Matthew, which begins with the birth of Christ and maintains a rootedness in the physical throughout its length.

Dominic had a strong sense of the goodness of God's creation —of life and nature—that would later be expressed brilliantly by St. Thomas Aquinas, who was transfixed by the idea that "we are made in the image of God." Preaching was a peaceful way to convey this. Unfortunately, the state of preaching at the time was abysmal, especially at the parish level. Cistercian monks were educated and were the first to be enlisted by Pope Alexander III in 1163, and later by the Third Lateran Council (1179), to answer the challenges raised by the Albigensians, but their whole style of life kept them out of cities, away from universities, out of the rough-and-tumble of theological debate.[14]

Dominic saw a glaring need for something different, an order that was educated but mobile—one versed in the theological controversies of the day and ready to respond in both word and example. Initially, he was not sure how this was going to work. He and his bishop, Diego, began preaching, but then the bishop soon died, leaving Dominic alone. He attracted followers, began a house in Toulouse, then went off to Rome in search of approval. His order was approved in 1216. Despite his obvious organizational skills,[15] Dominic probably did not foresee what direction his order would take. When he returned to the house in Toulouse, he informed the brothers that they would be dispersed, in twos, to spread the gospel. One of them famously balked at this and asked for more money before he would venture out into the world. But the friars, as they were now called, thinking that this would be fairly similar to other religious houses but with preaching as its primary ministry, were surprised at Dominic's command.

Thus, Francis of Assisi and Dominic set out to do their work in their different ways. The Dominicans began to preach a positive message of the goodness of God's creation, and Francis began to witness to this same message with his life. Francis wrote movingly about "Brother Sun and Sister Moon." He is the one who is credited with creating the first Christmas crèche.

65. Were women involved in these movements?

The majority of "perfects" in the Albigensian world were women. Riley-Smith claims that they made up 69 percent of the Albigensian faithful, and many of these came from the nobility.[16] Women tended to be treated better in the Albigensian world than in the orthodox Christian world, especially in the Albigensian care of widows and unmarried daughters. Women also rose more easily to positions of importance in the Albigensian world, although they could not become deacons or bishops. Dominic realized the significance of this and established a convent for women at Prouille, France, near Fanjeaux, in 1206, ten years before the men's order was approved. He had converted several Albigensian women to Christianity and needed a safe place for them to stay. Land was donated by laypeople eager to help, and the order of Dominican nuns was born.

Dominic wanted to channel the religious energy of these converts, most of whom were unmarried owing to their previous commitment to celibacy under Albigensianism. But he also wanted to provide a place for poor women who were being lured by the Albigensian promise of a free education.[17] He wanted to make sure that they stayed in the Catholic fold. These convents spread quickly throughout the western world.

Another monastery of nuns was founded in Assisi by Francis together with Clare of Assisi, a woman with whom Francis had a special relationship due to her affinity with his style of a life of poverty and prayer.[18]

66. But the Dominicans did not only preach against the Albigensians; they got involved in the Inquisition. How did this happen?

The pope was looking for a group of educated preachers who could address the issues being raised by the Albigensians. Previously, as we have seen (Q. 64), Cistercians were summoned to address these issues, and although they made some substantial preaching efforts among the Albigensians, they were not interested in abandoning their contemplative rigor on a permanent basis, and so some other solution was sought. Dominic provided the solution. Dominic's order had several advantages over previous religious models: although his was centralized in Rome, it was international in scope through a series of priors, provincials, and masters of the order who kept the houses and provinces interconnected. His men were educated, not unlike the Cistercians, but they were mobile. Dominic envisioned an order in which itinerant preachers could move from house to house, even from one province to another. The pope saw this as the perfect organization to accomplish what he wanted: the eradication of a heresy through persuasion and legislation. In an era when the pope was centralizing his political power in Rome, this was an order that was also centralizing its government in Rome, so the Dominicans seemed to fit the bill. The

Benedictine, Cistercian, and Carthusian monasteries, spread throughout the world, were remote, autonomous, and independent groups devoted to prayer, work, and study. The pope wanted some organization he could communicate with and from which he could expect a response. He found this in the Dominicans.

Dominic did not envision founding an order of canon lawyers and judges, so that it seems a bit strange that he would be enlisted to have his men involved in the Inquisition. It is mistaken, however, to think that the Inquisition was a court set up simply for the juridical eradication of heresy. Dominican inquisitors were there not to try and convict and punish so much as to persuade and absolve. Church courts were not places of trial and defense in our modern sense, but rather were places where the ignorant could be talked out of their error. Inquisitors spent much of their time instructing the accused about the error of their ways in hope that the accused would *not* be found guilty and sentenced, but would go free (if under some form of probation) and correct their ways.

67. So what was the Inquisition like? How was it organized?

One thing that needs to be remembered is that most Church trials were "inquisition trials," meaning that a tribunal (or three-some) of judges would hear a case, whether it be about probate of wills, divorce, or property rights, and all cases involving clerics. Only some of the cases heard by these courts were for heresy.[19] So one needs to distinguish between inquisition trials for nonheretical matters and inquisition trials for heresy. The inquisition *method* was standard by the thirteenth century.

Another distinction that needs to be made is that there were diocesan trials, held under the watchful eye of the local bishop, and papal trials, mandated and controlled by the pope. It is fair to say that most trials involving civil and criminal cases fell under the domain of the diocesan courts, while most trials for heresy fell under the papal system.

The method, when applied to heresy, was that a delegation

(usually three investigators or judges) would arrive in a town and "preach" the Inquisition, which meant explaining why heresy was so harmful and why people should come forward and give information about the activities and whereabouts of heretics.

Everyone—all males over the age of fourteen and females over the age of twelve—was required to sign an oath to support the Church, avoid heresy, and assist in the apprehension of heretics. Even the oath itself was a test, since Albigensians were forbidden to take oaths. The townspeople were given a grace period of six to ten days. If a person did not sign, he or she would be provisionally excommunicated. After one year, the person's excommunication would become official and a penal sentence would be added. Many people who knew they were strongly suspected of heresy would flee at this time.

68. Was the method and organization of the Medieval Inquisition different from that of the Spanish Inquisition?

The method was very much the same, but the goals of the two Inquisitions were, as we have seen (QQ. 52–53), very different, as was the organization. The Medieval Inquisition trials for heresy were largely controlled by the pope, with the assistance of local bishops. The Spanish Inquisition was driven by the crown without much reference to the pope at all. The pope, who demanded that he be able to oversee appointments of inquisitors and hear appeals of court decisions, was ignored. When the Spanish Inquisition began, the pope dismissed the Spanish ambassador to the Vatican. The Spaniards responded in kind, dismissing the Vatican ambassador to the Spanish court. It was the equivalent of severing diplomatic relations over a perceived and serious insult.

69. What were the time frames of these two Inquisitions?

The first known trial for heresy in the Middle Ages took place in 1022, when a group of eight priests who followed the

Albigensian doctrine had denied that creation came from God. This implied that the sacraments were useless at best and that marriage and sexual pleasure were sinful. One of these priests was confessor to the queen, so one can only imagine the king's interest in prosecuting him and his clerical friends. All eight were burned at the stake. But this was not, strictly speaking, an inquisition trial. Trials would gain more structure with time until the Medieval Inquisition was announced officially in 1234 and lasted, for all practical purposes, for one hundred years, when it essentially ran out of victims. The combination of crusade, preaching, and trial had accomplished its work. The inquisition method would remain in place, and is still in place today, as Church tribunals essentially use the same procedure: evidence (of marital incompatibility, for example) is brought to a tribunal of judges, who examine the evidence and make a decision.

The Spanish Inquisition began in 1481 and lasted officially until 1834, when it was shut down for good by order of the crown. But most of its work was done in the first one hundred years, much like the Medieval Inquisition.

70. Why was a tribunal of judges deemed to be the best method of conducting a trial?

In order to ensure fairness, a tribunal consisted of three judges. One judge alone, obviously, could be a tyrant. Three judges acted as checks and balances to one another and supplied alternative positions and solutions. Reports would be sent to Rome about the conduct of fellow judges, complaining of their cruelty or lack of respect for the accused. It is also possible that the accused might find sympathy from one of the judges.

71. What were the responsibilities of these judges?

They did everything. They gathered information about who might be accused, assessed the seriousness of the charges, decided who would be the witnesses both for and against, heard the case, and then pronounced judgment and a sentence if one was called for. This is very different from our judicial system (outside of courts martial, which are surprisingly like the medieval system), where a jury of one's peers assesses the information given to them by an outside source and passes judgment. The judge merely presides over the trial and ensures that the procedure is fair and then, having been given the verdict, pronounces judgment and possibly sentences those found guilty (again, at the recommendation of the jury). Modern judges may reduce sentences or monetary settlements if they think such decisions are exorbitant, but they are always guided by the desires of the jury. There was no jury in inquisition trials.

72. Was there a method by which the importance of the cases was graduated?

One of the things the judges needed to determine was the *degree of heresy* involved: some were more serious than others. People who aided or concealed heretics were considered to be heretics themselves, though the nature and extent of their involvement had to be determined by the court. Then there were those who showed an interest in heresy by attending meetings, speaking with known heretics, or taking part in ceremonies. The worst offenders were active heretics themselves: those who preached heresy, believed in the heresy, and encouraged others to join their groups.

This is one of the significant contributions of the Inquisition to modern law. Cases were first heard in a preliminary manner to determine whether the information justified a trial or not. This was called the *inquisitio generalis,* or "general inquisition," which determined whether some form of heresy had taken place, whether it was worth pursuing, and whether the accused was "triable." Today we would call this a grand jury. If the person was deemed to be triable and his or her offense significant, the *inquisitio particularis,* or "particular inquisition," began.

73. Once a person of interest was identified and the level of his involvement in heresy determined, how did the trial proceed?

Ideally, as today, the judges hoped for an admission of guilt. Such admissions saved time, and the accused was usually given a lighter sentence. If the accused did not admit guilt, judges gained information from witnesses, spies planted in prisons, or tests. A typical test would be the offer to take an oath or to eat some meat, the acceptance of which might clear the accused. One man pleaded, "Lords, hear me, I am no heretic, for I have a wife and lie with her, and have children. And I eat flesh and lie and swear, and am a faithful Christian."[20]

Only two types of proof were recognized: partial and full proof. Only full proof could convict. Proof was regarded as full when the accused confessed, if the accused was caught in the act, or if there were two witnesses to a heretical act. All other evidence was considered to be partial proof, and no amount of partial proof could add up to full proof. However, if a great body of partial proof, or what we would call today "circumstantial evidence," had accumulated, torture might be used to extract a confession.

74. Torture and the Inquisition are almost synonymous. Was torture used in questioning a suspect? How extensive was its use?

Torture against heretics was indeed authorized by the pope in the year 1250. Its use was limited to those seriously suspect of heresy but whose evidence did not amount to full proof (see Q. 73). The application of torture was by no means limited to Church courts or against heretics. The techniques used in torturing prisoners were the standard means in practice at the time: denial of food and water, denial of visits from family, being tied to the rack or chained to prison walls in ways that limited motion, and so forth. The Spanish introduced the *strapado*, which was a particularly heinous torture in which the prisoner's hands were tied behind his back and to another rope, from which he was dropped, resulting in dislocation and excruciating pain to the shoulders.

The usefulness of torture was questioned even then. Tortured prisoners may tell their torturers only what they want to hear. And sometimes torture could be applied to get the prisoner to confess to something he or she did not do.[21]

75. If the charges were graduated, were the sentences graduated as well?

The sentences corresponded to the seriousness of the charges as well as to the frequency of convictions. Much as in modern trial procedure, a convicted person's record might be cited by the judge in the sentencing procedure. A first-time offender would not be punished nearly as severely as a repeat offender. This was true in the Medieval Inquisition as well. Sentences were not so much punitive as educational, or warnings of worse to come if the behavior were to continue. The harshest punishments were meted out to recalcitrant preachers or practitioners of heresy, people who were found guilty one year and found to be guilty again several years later. But it was certainly the case that lesser charges merited lesser sentences.

76. Could you give some examples of typical sentences?

Ninety percent of the sentences passed down by the Inquisition courts were canonical, that is, Church-related. These sentences actually resemble penances that might have been given out in confession for sins committed. Certain penalties were imposed, such as fasting, pilgrimage to a local or distant shrine, increased attendance at Mass, the wearing of distinctive clothing or badges, or acts of charity—what we would call "community service." Priests could be suspended from public ministry (saying public Mass, hearing confession, preaching, and so forth). A friar could be placed in a prison cell within his convent, a sentence that was known as an *In Pace*, from the phrase *Requiescat in pace*: "May he rest in peace." It involved severe solitary confinement, with visits from a friend permitted only once a month. House arrest, as in the case of Galileo, was given with permission (in his case) to keep working on his projects. In the Roman Inquisition, founded in 1588, even life sentences meant parole after a few years, usually three.

More serious sentences would involve banishment from a particular locale for prescribed periods of time, prison sentences (again, of various lengths), and burning at the stake. The Spanish sentenced serious offenders to time on their galleys, which was often a death sentence.

77. Were all the decisions made in court, or did some "out-of-court" settlements occur?

Similar to our own out-of-court settlements, where an accused party would reach an agreement with the court, usually with a reduced sentence in mind, the Inquisition allowed and even encouraged these in high-visibility cases. In the Roman Inquisition, former priests and sometimes well-known theologians who had apostatized (that is, become Protestant) and wished to be reconciled to their former faith would negotiate a quiet return through members of their religious order. One of the most famous of these is that of Bernardino Ochino, the apostate minister general of the newly founded Capuchin branch of the Franciscan order, who was sought out by Ignatius of Loyola with a view to reconciling him to the Church while bypassing the judicial process of the Inquisition.[22]

78. Can you tell me about the sentence of distinctive clothing and badges? What was this?

Wearing a distinctive robe or, more usually, a cross of some color, was a way of telling the community that the wearer had been convicted of heresy in some (probably not a great) degree. This was worn for a period of time such as one or two years, and then the sentence would be revoked for "good behavior." But life could be difficult while the person wore the garment: that person was to be shunned and his or her company avoided. This stigma made it difficult for the convicted to function normally in society, to purchase and sell goods at market, and so forth. People would not want to associate with someone convicted by the Inquisition, so friends could be lost and one's children stigmatized as well.

79. Why would going on pilgrimage be a sentence and a hardship? Didn't people want to go on pilgrimage?

Yes, if they could afford it. Pilgrimages could be very rewarding spiritually (which was why they were imposed as sentences), but they could also be time-consuming, expensive, and dangerous, depending on the distance from one's home and the land to be traveled through. Again, the distance of the shrine site to be visited reflected the severity of the "crime."

Proofs of pilgrimage came in the form of a medal or glass souvenir of some kind, obtained at the pilgrimage site and then returned and shown to the parish priest as proof that the person had fulfilled the sentence or penance. The shrine at Compostela in northern Spain famously had (and still has) a seashell as its medal. Cologne Cathedral, where the bones of the Three Kings are supposedly enshrined, had a medal featuring the Blessed Mother but with the prominent presence of the Magi. The pilgrim wore these on the journey as proof that he or she was on the way or had visited the shrine site, with a sense of pride in having accomplished a difficult feat, but also as protection on the way. Attacking a pilgrim was considered a very serious crime, far beyond the simple robbing of a traveler.

80. How many people were sentenced during the Medieval Inquisition? And how many were executed?

This is difficult to say and is now the subject of intense research. There are some amazingly complete statistics, including transcripts of actual trials, such as that of Joan of Arc (see Q. 83), and a lot of data on the number of accused, convictions, sentences, and so forth.

In 1245 and the years following, inquisitors took 420 depositions in Le Mas-Saintes-Puelles, a small town known for a high incidence of heresy, and were able to find the names of only seven people who had received the Cathar form of baptism in the previous thirty-five years. In Fanjeaux, a larger town with an even larger reputation for heresy, only twenty-six names were found. In Beziers, a city of about ten thousand people, the bishop in 1209 drew up a list of those who were found guilty of some level of heresy: 220.[23] Edward Peters contends that "the fury and indiscriminate tactics of earlier figures like Conrad of Marburg are gone."[24] The Inquisition essentially ended the pyromania and mob violence of the Albigensian Crusade.

Of the 930 guilty verdicts handed down by the Dominican Bernardo Gui, who was probably the most active inquisitor of the age (he was active as an inquisitor from 1308 to 1323), only forty-two were given over to "the secular arm" for execution.

81. How extensive and how reliable are the records of the Medieval Inquisition?

Many records have been lost, though not through any deliberate culling on the part of the Church. The Church wanted the records kept, after all. Records were lost over the years for many reasons, including attacks on traveling inquisitors (for which their proceedings and lists of names, rather than their persons, were the object of attack), the obvious results of fires and floods on archives, and the ravages of such events as the French Revolution and Spanish secularization, where anything related to the church was subject to destruction.

82. Was the burning of witches, often associated with the Medieval Inquisition, a common occurrence?

Witchcraft was an umbrella term for a number of practices, including superstition, necromancy (communication with the dead), black magic, and the casting of spells. In fact, the majority of those tried for witchcraft in the Roman Inquisition were men (60 percent). Magic, especially the black arts as they were called, grew in popularity into the fourteenth and fifteenth centuries and became the object of Roman legislation. In 1484, the pope issued a bull against witches entitled *Summis Desiderantes affectibus*, which ordered the Inquisition to investigate people accused of witchcraft. This led to the writing, in 1487, of a commentary famously called *Malleus Maleficarum* (the "Hammer of Witches") by two Dominicans. According to F. Merzbacher, trials for witchcraft reached their climax in the first third of the sixteenth century.[25] But here the trail becomes murky as Protestants joined in with their own trials against witchcraft, the most notorious being the Salem witch trials in the Massachusetts Bay Colony in the late seventeenth century, where twenty "witches"—seven of them men—were burned in one summer.

This may be difficult for us, in the twenty-first century, to grasp. But is it? While we hear mostly of "white witches," we also delight in Hollywood's ventures into the world of dark powers and the occult, with the popular television series *Buffy the Vampire Slayer* and the Harry Potter books and movies being two good examples. Even the loveable *Wizard of Oz* featured a good witch and a bad witch, the latter of whom was quite horrifying to a five-year-old. While this, for us, may serve as entertainment and escape, in the late Middle Ages it was taken more seriously and needed to be addressed more seriously. The renegade Dominican Giordano Bruno seriously suggested that the secret to world peace in 1600 was to be found in having magicians serve as advisors to kings and rulers. He cited Copernicus as his source, which managed to get both Bruno and Galileo into trouble (see Q. 101).

In any case, numbers are hard to come by. We know that, in the seventeenth century, the tribunal of Toledo during the Spanish Inquisition handled 151 cases of witchcraft. That is, on average, 1.5

cases per year—hardly a "witch hunt." And some of these cases could be for minor offenses. Once again, the people who were executed were repeat offenders, not first-time dabblers in the occult.

83. Why was Joan of Arc, no doubt one of the most famous persons to be tried by the Inquisition, tried as a heretic?

Joan of Arc led the forces of France against the English during the Hundred Years' War and managed to have the French king Charles VII crowned in Reims Cathedral. This was her dream all along. She was taken prisoner near Compiegne in 1430 and sold by the duke of Burgundy to the English. She was tried in Rouen by the bishop of Beauvais as a heretic (that is, a witch) on the grounds that she dressed like a man (a soldier) and heard voices. While in prison she resumed wearing male attire, which was a sign of a relapse. On May 31, 1431, she was burned at the stake in Rouen. She was nineteen years old.

Dominican inquisitors, who were present but not involved in the trial, complained about her treatment, and Pope Callistus established an appellate court to examine the case. She was declared innocent in 1456 and was canonized in 1920.[26]

84. What sort of pleas did the accused typically make during their trials?

Pleas varied, depending on the enthusiasm of the accused. Some (few) confessed and defied the court. Joan of Arc frequently told the judge that he had asked her that before, or that she had taken an oath before and was not going to go through that again. Others confessed and threw themselves at the mercy of the court, hoping for a lighter sentence. Many pleaded ignorance. These are among the most common pleas:

"I did not know what was going on."

"I did not know that those people were heretics."

"I was at a Cathar meal and 'adored' the Cathars [that is, listened to them with attention], but then left early—claiming to be sick—when I heard what they were saying."

"I participated in the rites, but then my brother-in-law and I left and went to Mass."

"I do not know what happened when my brother became a heretic, because I was guarding the door."

"I did not know what happened when my father became a heretic because I was deaf at the time."

"I only took part in the ceremony because [an official of the city] was there and I thought I'd better go along."[27]

85. How were the sentences carried out? Was there a public ceremony?

When the investigations were complete (sessions typically would not last more than two weeks), the inquisitors, in a solemn ceremony attended by the townspeople, civic officials, clergy, and nobility, pronounced judgment. This ceremony was known as an auto-da-fé in Spain—a confession of faith. The ranking inquisitor preached a short sermon, then pronounced sentence on the recalcitrant, or "repeat offenders," beginning with the most serious crimes and proceeding to those accused of less serious crimes. (This process was reversed in Spain.) The most serious would be "handed over to the secular arm" for execution. Sometimes the dead were ordered to be exhumed and their bones burned. Those who had fled before trial would be officially excommunicated. Then those who had been "paroled" by previous trials might be released from their penalties.

86. Were there abuses in the Inquisition system?

Of course there were abuses with the Inquisition. There are problems with every judicial system, including our own in the twenty-first century. I think it is best to divide up the various "problems" into two categories: problems and abuses.

Problems first:

1. Religious orders were nervous about their men participating in an inquisition trial. These men became a separate caste and might regard themselves as above the rule of a local superior. Their visits could disrupt community life.
2. Bishops did not always appreciate the appearance of the Inquisition. The bishop, after all, had to stay behind and live with the people who might not be too happy with the proceedings. But even more, he might resent the interference of a religious order in the workings of his diocese. Bishops, after all, have historically had a rather nervous relationship with religious orders, whose members are more independent than their own diocesan clergy. In 1279, for example, the bishop of Padua was reprimanded by Pope Nicholas III for not cooperating with the visiting friars.
3. There were rivalries between the religious orders involved, especially between the Dominicans and the Franciscans. Members of one order might use the Inquisition to get rid of members of the other order. In 1266, the Dominicans of Marseilles brought false witnesses against the Franciscans. Eventually one pope, the Franciscan Sixtus IV (1471–84), legislated that members of one religious order could not use the Inquisition to try members of another religious order.[28]
4. Sometimes the people could be hostile. Several inquisitors were murdered, the most notable being the Dominican Peter of Verona (Peter Martyr) on his way from Como to Milan. In 1242, following increased activity by the Inquisition, eleven people were murdered in several attacks in southern France, as many as eight of whom were inquisitors. (This attack backfired, as the assailants were tracked to their stronghold at Montségur and executed. Thus the Cathars lost their stronghold, their hierarchy, and their most enthusiastic leaders.)

Part of the reason for attacking inquisitors had less to do with revenge than with obtaining the records they might be holding.

Second, abuses:

1. Overzealous and "freelance" inquisitors occasionally overstepped their authority. Conrad of Marburg was notoriously cruel and was eventually murdered by the populace. In one outrageous case in 1239, Robert the Bugre, a Dominican who was a converted Cathar, sentenced 180 heretics, including the bishop, to death in Montwiner. His own order suspended him from his office as inquisitor and sentenced him to life in prison.

2. Politicians could use the Inquisition to target political opponents rather than religious extremists, often with property in mind. Since part of a capital sentence was the confiscation of property, this could prove a tempting target indeed. It must be noted that the confiscation of property was usually dispensed from.

3. Occasionally a dead person would be tried and sentenced for heresy—again usually with property in mind. Gerardo of Florence was tried sixty years after he had died. While this may seem, at first blush, to be vindictive, inhuman, and barbaric, we must remember those states in the supposedly more enlightened United States of America of the early twenty-first century that have lifted statutes of limitations so that priests, long dead and thus incapable of defending themselves, could be tried and sued for sexual abuses. In California, where the statute of limitations in abuse cases was completely lifted for one year, one could theoretically have sued the Franciscan order for some criminal act allegedly committed by Junipero Serra in 1770. Inquisition abuses are not as different as we would like them to be.

4. False accusations could be made by personal enemies.

87. Did safeguards of any kind exist to prevent problems from arising and abuses from happening?

Safeguards certainly existed but were not always effective. The tribunal system was a safeguard insofar as inquisitors were answerable to one another. Interestingly, inquisitors were subject to the same rules they used on those suspected of heresy. Allegations against inquisitors for unfair treatment could also be made anonymously. Bernardo Gui was quite meticulous in ensuring the fair treatment of heretics. His guidelines for inquisitors included the following instructions:

Be diligent for the truth.

Do not be given either to anger or to laziness.

Always be open to appeals for delay or lesser sentences.

Be merciful, honest, consistent, and not cruel.

Never start trouble, but do not back off if someone else starts trouble.

Do not believe something simply because it is likely.

Do not disbelieve something because it is unlikely.[29]

When I read these guidelines to an audience at the Smithsonian Institution in Washington, D.C., an FBI agent approached me after the talk and said that those guidelines were amazingly similar to the guidelines demanded of its agents by the FBI!

In addition to internal checks, the pope also monitored complaints and issued directives in an attempt to correct abuses.

88. Could you give a summary of the Medieval Inquisition?

Inquisition trials for heresy in the Middle Ages were mostly confined to southern France and northern Italy. Scandinavian countries escaped them entirely. England saw almost no trials for heresy, the trial of Joan of Arc (on English soil in what is now France) being a notable exception. Most of France and Spain saw little Inquisition activity, in the case of Spain until the late 1400s.

Trials for heresy began to recede significantly by the year 1330, mostly for lack of suspects or, as one author suggested mischievously, because of "an eventual shortage of combustible material."[30]

Several factors combined to eradicate heresy in the thirteenth century: the Albigensian Crusade, followed on by the preaching of the friars and papal legislation.

As far as the treatment of criminals goes, the Medieval Inquisition made considerable advances, many of which can still be seen in trial procedures today: the pretrial hearings, graduation of crimes and sentences, manuals that provided judges with guidance in investigation and sentencing (we call them sentencing guidelines today), admonitions to investigators to be fair, safeguards against unfair behavior (mistrials), and provisions for the accused to defend themselves and make appeals to the pope in cases of perceived mis-carriages of justice.

89. While admitting that the Medieval Inquisition was productive of many advances in judicial procedures, why does it still continue to upset modern critics, and why did Pope John Paul II apologize for it in 1994?

There are three main reasons why the Inquisition (both Medieval and Spanish) continues to draw criticism:

1. It is a dangerous thing to accuse people of what they *believe* or are *thinking*. In the Middle Ages, sins against reason were considered more serious than sins of the flesh. Dante names the most serious sinners as those who defraud, lie, believe in heresy, or betray—all rational acts rather than acts of passion —and places them in the deepest levels of his Inferno. Modern sensibilities are repelled at the idea that one's thoughts can be the subject of persecution. Queen Mary Tudor (Bloody Mary) executed 282 people for heresy, which made her unpopular; her successor, Queen Elizabeth I, learned this lesson and executed far more than 282

people, but for treason, which was more acceptable to the public. Pope John Paul II, in apologizing for the Inquisition, cited Vatican II, which stated, "The truth cannot impose itself except by virtue of its own truth, as it wins over the mind with both gentleness and power."[31]

2. Religion was taken far more seriously in the Middle Ages than it is today and was part of the very fabric of society. Public holidays and celebrations centered around the feast days of the Church. It is necessary for us to contextualize this and realize that threats against the Church—of which Albigensianism was certainly one—threatened the very existence of society.

3. The use of torture in investigations, while used in both civil and ecclesiastical courts in the Middle Ages, continues to repel us.

90. Just when it seemed that the Medieval Inquisition had run its course and come, for the most part, to an end, the Inquisition suddenly arose again in Spain. Why did the Spanish Inquisition begin?

The Spanish Inquisition was intended to aid in the unification of Spain. For centuries the military crusade known as the Reconquista had steadily pushed Muslim rulers to the south, eventually isolating them in their last stronghold of Granada. By then Christian Spain comprised two kingdoms, Aragon and Castile. Ferdinand, heir to the throne of Aragon, and Isabella, queen of Castile, married in 1469. Ferdinand's succession to the throne in 1479 effectively united the two kingdoms. When Granada fell to the Christians in 1492, the unification was complete.

Or was it? There were two main groups of people in Spain who were not Christian—Jews and Muslims—and their conformity to Christianity was considered essential to the unification of the country. On January 2, 1492, the last Muslim of Granada surrendered

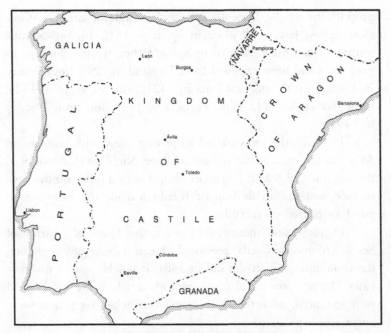

MAP 3: THE SPANISH INQUISITION

to the combined forces of Ferdinand and Isabella. By March 31, they decreed that Jews and Muslims still living in Spain would have to convert to Christianity or leave the country in four months. About one third of the Jewish population, of which Henry Kamen estimates the total to have been eighty thousand, fled the country, mostly to Eastern Europe.[32] The other two thirds converted and were known as *conversos*. (Muslims who converted were known as *moriscos*.) Suspicion fell on some of these converts, who became known as Judaizers,[33] for reverting to Jewish rituals in secret.

Part of the concern about Judaizers involved several schemes concerning Muslims in Africa who were planning to reinvade the Iberian Peninsula. If only a few *conversos* were implicated in these plots, a panicky suspicion fell on the whole group.

Along with this went the age-old prejudices against Jews generally, especially among the lower classes. This reached epidemic proportions in the fifteenth century throughout Europe. While riots against Jews took place in Spain in 1412–14, anti-Semitic sentiment was not restricted to Spain; rather, it had a long pedigree. Jews had been expelled from England in 1290, from France in 1306, from Vienna and Linz in 1421, from Cologne in 1424, from Bavaria in 1442, from Perugia in 1485, and from Tuscany in 1494.

In Spain, the crown tried to protect the Jewish population. Also, the Church, in the person of Pope Nicholas II, denounced the exclusion of Jewish Christians from political office on the basis of race, and the archbishop of Toledo forbade the existence of guilds organized on racial lines.

Despite these measures, however, the Dominican prior of Seville (Alonso de Ojeda) pressured Queen Isabella into beginning the Inquisition, which she did in 1481. It quickly spread to other cities. The first auto-da-fé (the ceremony at which the condemned were executed) occurred in the same year, when six people were burnt. Ojeda preached.

91. How violent was the Spanish Inquisition in its first years?

The initial stages of the Inquisition in Spain were its most violent, but even here modern historians urge caution. As Helen Rawlings points out:

> [The statistics show that] the holocausts of the 1480s were short-lived. For most of its active history the execution rate remained below 2 percent—an average of five people per year. Torture and the death penalty were only rarely applied—almost exclusively during the early years of its existence.[34]

Later on, as we will see, modern Jewish historians have discovered that, although one hundred persons would be sentenced to death in the Spanish Inquisition, only one or two would be executed, and the rest were hung in effigy.[35]

Jewish historians are divided about the extent of the Judaizing tendencies of *conversos*. Benzion Netanyahu in *The Origins of the Inquisition* regards the establishment of the Inquisition as clearly an anti-Semitic move on the part of the crown, eager to benefit from lower-class prejudices, eager to eliminate even Jews who had become devout Christians. However, both Haim Beinart (*Records of the Trials of the Spanish Inquisition in Ciudad Real 1483–85*) and Yitzhak Baer (*A History of the Jews in Christian Spain*) view the Inquisition as more a sociological phenomenon than something essentially anti-Semitic.[36] Both Beinart and Baer agree that the inquisitors were correct in suspecting that the *conversos* were Judaizers.[37]

92. Did the Spanish Inquisition target people who were not Jewish or Muslim converts?

Besides wanting Spaniards to conform to Catholicism, the crown wanted to use the Inquisition to reform Catholicism. After 1540, 60 percent of those tried by the Inquisition in Spain were "old Catholics," that is, Catholics by birth. They could be charged with *delitos menores* (minor crimes), which included a range of offenses from heretical propositions (outbursts against the faith or bad theology) to superstition, blasphemy, or sexual offenses (such as bigamy, homosexuality, bestiality, or solicitation from the confessional).

Even Catholics who are today greatly revered by the Catholic Church as saints were "victims" of the Inquisition. Ignatius Loyola, the founder of the Society of Jesus or the Jesuits, was imprisoned four times for suspicious writings (including parts of his Spiritual Exercises) or being an *alumbrado* (an "enlightened one" and a euphemism that could mean a "charismatic," in the sense of a layperson who feels a calling to preach and direct others in spiritual matters, or a Protestant). Teresa of Avila was accused of misconduct and one of her books placed on the Index of Forbidden Books.

93. Were Protestants ever targets of the Spanish Inquisition?

Because the Spanish kings were also the Holy Roman Emperors, they were especially attuned to the problems brought about in Germany (the Holy Roman Empire) by Martin Luther, who would publically defy the papacy by posting his 95 Theses in 1517 and then be excommunicated in 1521. After 1520, we see Lutherans appearing on Inquisition lists under Major Heresies (as opposed to minor crimes) along with *conversos* and *moriscos*. The king did not want the situation in Germany to repeat itself in Spain, with princes siding or not siding with Luther in a match that would later end in the Thirty Years' War and permanently divide Germany along denominational lines. However, most of those charged with Lutheranism (which was an umbrella term for Protestants, including Calvinists) were foreigners. The Reformation never really made inroads among the native Spanish, and those Spanish who were interested in Reformation movements generally left the country.[38]

94. So, all told, how many victims did the Spanish Inquisition claim?

The first few years were the worst by far. Local tribunals were loosely organized and did not keep good records; they could also be more violent. If Kamen's estimates are correct (see Q. 88), then the one third of the Jewish population who fled the country should be counted as victims, while fifty to sixty thousand Jews remained as *conversos*, not all of whom, however, were victims. Kamen concludes that, even if *all* of them were executed by the Inquisition, and they clearly were not, then the statistics *still* need to be dramatically reduced. The popular notion that there were 400,000 victims of the Spanish Inquisition is obviously a gross exaggeration.

Up to 1530, at most about two thousand were sent to the stake, with fifteen thousand being reconciled (disciplined) in some way short of execution.[39] After 1540, attention on the Jewish converts waned. Between 1540 and 1700, in all jurisdictions of the

Inquisition, 826 people were executed. This was 1.8 percent of all those convicted. In other words, after 1540, the Inquisition executed very few people. The district of Valencia killed almost as many people in its first fifty years as did all twenty jurisdictions in the next 150 years. Ironically, as the Inquisition became more organized, the number of its victims fell dramatically. Thus, numbers of the executed range from two thousand to five thousand.

95. How well organized was the Spanish Inquisition?

Initially, as was discussed previously, it was not very well organized. With time, it became one of the most organized (though not most efficient) governmental agencies on record.

The organization was three-tiered. At the top was the Supreme Council, called "The Council of the Supreme and General Inquisition," or *La Suprema*. It had eight councilors and the Inquisitor General. Below that were twenty-one tribunals, or courts delegated to hear cases regionally, corresponding to the major cities of Spain and the New World. Below that were functionaries such as lawyers, theologians, and secretaries. Once this organization began to function, the Spaniards kept meticulous records that reveal not only the extent of the Inquisition (for example, numbers and types of accusations and penalties), but also a social history that goes way beyond the domain of a trial for heresy. These records could include a brief biographical sketch of the accused, a genealogy (whether there were Jews in the person's ancestry—and here the accused often could not remember very much about his grandparents and beyond), and the social context in which the accused was arrested. Was the accused literate, educated?

We must remember that the inquisitors kept such good records because they thought they were doing good and were not about to conceal anything. Good records made for the saving of time and protected the inquisitors from charges of unfairness.

The number of records still extant is staggering. One author commented, "The system of recording adopted by the *Suprema* was a masterpiece of archival science."[40] In Toledo alone, six thousand trials are recorded that span the entire 356-year length of the Spanish Inquisition. The *Suprema*'s archive now belongs to the state archive and comprises 1,115 volumes of manuscripts and 4,000 bundles of loose papers tied together. Up to 1820, fourteen or fifteen archives still existed intact. Then five more archives were destroyed in 1820 in uprisings against the government. In Valencia, the Inquisition papers ended up in a fireworks factory, where they were used in the construction of fireworks. Mexico's archives are preserved intact.

Obviously, the Spanish Inquisition encompassed Spanish territory outside of Spain, especially in the New World. One can still see an inquisitor's residence and jail (across the street) in Mexico in San Miguel de Allende. They were temporary quarters.

96. Did inquisitors have books of instructions to guide them?

With the advent of printing, handbooks abounded that provided inquisitors with guides as to how to identify heresy, how to expose it, and how to deal with it. It also provided inquisitors with sentencing guidelines, a very modern concept indeed. First offenders were treated mildly, second offenders more severely. The seriousness of the offense also determined the seriousness of the sentence.

One such typical extant handbook begins by asking, "How is the Faith to be Violated?"[41] One realizes early on that the author must be a Dominican in the way he meticulously sets out distinctions; St. Thomas, after all, stated, "Never deny, seldom affirm, always distinguish" when addressing theological questions.

The answer begins:

> The Catholic faith can be violated in two ways, negatively (or privately), and positively. The faith is violated in a negative or private way when anyone does not know those things (matters of faith) that as a Catholic he should know, or when anyone disregards those

things that he is bound to do in accordance with the good and favor of faith. Positively, by doing that which is opposed in any way to the faith: and this can happen in two ways, namely directly and indirectly.[42]

The handbook continues by distinguishing levels of heresy. Let me give some examples (the numbers correspond to the numbers in the book):

4. The first level belongs to heretical statement. A heretical statement is censured when it is clearly opposed or is contrary or contradictory to some truth, about which it is certainly clear that it deals with the faith.

9. The second level belongs to erroneous statement, certainly one that is opposed to truth not pertaining to the truth of the faith through a certain theological certitude, and is held by clear inference from revealed truth where it is contained as something distinct.

15. The sixth level belongs to a scandalous statement. And such a statement supplies a reason or occasion of scandal concerning some doctrine or truth of the faith.

23. The eleventh level is a blasphemous or slanderous statement, namely, one that asserts harmful things to God or the saints by attributing those things to them which are not fitting, or by denying things that are owed.[43]

Such handbooks had the effect of informing inquisitors about their duties and the limits of their power, assisting them in identifying heretics as well as the level of their heresy. It also standardized sentencing procedures, so that those who were sentenced would not think themselves treated differently from others.

97. When did the Spanish Inquisition end?

Again, the first years saw the most intense and fearsome activity. After 1540, trials began to concentrate more on the morals of Catholics rather than on the faith of converts. After 1600, the influence of the Inquisition was clearly on the wane. There would be bursts of activity or attempts to assert its authority—as when 165

Judaizers were executed (the vast majority in Castille) between 1721 and 1725—but the crown increasingly lost interest. The last person executed was in 1781 when a misguided woman claimed to have made contact with the Blessed Virgin and to have freed millions of souls from purgatory.[44]

The effectiveness of the Spanish Inquisition was long over after the first decade of the eighteenth century, and for the rest of the century its continuance would be challenged by liberals and Enlightenment thinkers as a symbol of backwardness and defended by the Spanish bishops as the only hope of Catholicism in Spain. By this time, however, its impact on the country was over, and the Spanish Inquisition officially ended in 1834, by decree of the queen regent of Spain. It had lasted 356 years.

98. What do recent scholars make of the Spanish Inquisition?

Surprising results have emerged from recent research. Obviously, the numbers of victims needs to be reduced dramatically. The popular number of 400,000 victims is now seen to be as preposterous. The use and extent of torture and execution is far less than was thought, according to current research. Kamen estimated that roughly 1 percent of those sentenced to death were executed, while the rest were hung in effigy as a warning.[45] Torture was used far less often than in secular courts.

Another finding is that the Spanish Inquisition was not the monolithic, efficiently organized pogrom that it has been portrayed to be. Rather, it seems to have been quite inefficient (especially in its early stages) and porous in its enforcement. For example, ports through which Lutheran preachers and writings came into Spain could hardly be policed efficiently. Even in the United States of post–2001 terrorism, only 2 percent of the containers coming into American ports are screened.[46] Henry Kamen concludes that the Inquisition could not possibly have enforced control at the ports or points of entry into the country. The Pyrenees frontier was essentially an open border, and "the bookshops of Barcelona were filled with books printed in France."[47]

99. Was the Spanish Inquisition used to eliminate political opponents?

There were a few high-profile cases in which this happened. The Dominican archbishop of Toledo, Bartolomé Carranza, who had written a catechism approved by the Council of Trent, found his book condemned in Spain. But the issue was not about his catechism; it was about the fact that he had been appointed to the most important diocese in Spain (Toledo) over the heads of Fernando de Valdes, the Inquisitor General and archbishop of Seville, and Pedro de Castro, the bishop of Cuenca, both aristocrats who resented the low-born Carranza. It did not help Carranza that Melchior Cano, his religious brother in the Dominican order and a theological star, was also his longtime enemy. Cano charged Carranza with making statements that were "scandalous, rash and ill-sounding, some with savor of heresy, others which are erroneous, and even some which are heretical."[48] Archbishop Carranza spent eight years in prison (1559–67) for writing the catechism. Then he went to Rome and was imprisoned there for another nine years. He was finally freed and died a few days later at Santa Maria Sopra Minerva.[49]

Another case against Francis Borgia, "the best-known Jesuit in Spain," was highly charged with politics. Borgia had irked the Inquisitor General by having his (Borgia's) name invoked in the defense of Carranza. In addition, King Philip did not like Borgia (or the Jesuits, for that matter). Borgia had been rumored at court to have been living in concubinage with King Philip's sister, Juana. And the Jesuits were continually lobbying to have the Spanish crown support their college in Rome, much to the king's annoyance. Borgia fled to Portugal and then to Rome to escape condemnation. He died in Rome in 1572 as superior general of the Jesuits. Nonetheless, his book *Obras del Cristiano* was placed on the Spanish Index of Forbidden Books, which was separate from the Roman list.[50]

100. Galileo's treatment cannot go unmentioned. Why was he tried by the Inquisition? Was his treatment fair?

Galileo was a good friend of the pope and had the best telescope in the world, and he used to let the pope look through it. Galileo got into trouble for two reasons: first, he claimed things for science that seemed to question certain assertions about God derived from the Bible, and second, his career followed shortly upon that of Giordano Bruno, a Dominican friar who was executed for heresy.

Let us go to the first problem. Like most scientists of the time, Galileo was thoroughly Christian and saw his science as affecting theology. This is what got him into trouble. If he had just reported what he saw, I believe he would have been allowed to carry on with his research. But he felt the need to write about the implications of what he saw—for theology. He was not really prepared to do that.[51] The Church, also, was not prepared to absorb quickly everything Galileo was finding; it wanted time to sift the evidence. Galileo was not giving it time. The Catholic Church was reeling from charges by the Protestant world that it was not biblically oriented, did not consider the Bible that important, and so forth. Every assault on Catholicism by Protestant thinkers was based on the assumption that the Bible alone—*sola scriptura*—was the basis for authority. All of a sudden, a real scientist came forward and proclaimed that the Genesis story of creation, the *biblical* story of creation, might not be scientifically accurate. So the Catholic Church, under fire from two sources—the fundamental Protestants and the modern scientists—felt itself in need of slowing down the process. The one person they could get at—and slow down—was Galileo. So they did.

The other problem for Galileo was Giordano Bruno. Bruno claimed Copernicus as his original source but was then taking the Copernican claim that the sun was the center of the universe to another level and maintaining that God (in some astronomical way) was the center of the universe. He was blending real observation with spiritual speculation of a rather bizarre sort. Bruno was also claiming that magic was the solution to world peace, and that kings and emperors needed only to surround themselves with magicians as consultants to advise them about the best course to world peace. Bruno attracted the notice of the Venetian Inquisition, another judicial body that prided itself on being separate from Rome but that released Bruno as being a harmless crackpot. But Bruno continued to preach his message and found himself in the Roman Inquisition courts. He was burned at the stake after refusing to retract his absurd claims.

The problem for Galileo was not that he liked or supported Bruno; it was that he also cited Copernicus as his authoritative source, which was the same source cited by Bruno. One might say it was a case of very bad timing. Someone needed to divorce Copernicus from the strange Bruno, but Galileo did not see the need to do that. History and science, thus, have conveniently remembered the findings of Galileo and forgotten about the history of Giordano Bruno and the dilemma that the Church found itself in.

The modern world wants an immediate reaction to the latest findings of scientific research. That was not the case in 1600. As exciting as Galileo's findings were, the Church wanted time to evaluate what his discoveries were leading to, time to process the evidence, and time to ponder the consequences. I believe that the Church was right to temper Galileo's enthusiasm at what were exciting new discoveries. Not all of Galileo's findings were accurate—the sun, after all, does *not* seem to be the center of the universe. The Church authorities ordered him simply not to publish, but he continued to do so, violating the order. Thus he was arrested and placed under house confinement and allowed to continue his research but not to publish his findings. He was never imprisoned or tortured, as the graphic paintings of Francisco Goya indicate.

101. If the Inquisition made such advances in trial procedure, then why does it have the terrible reputation it has today?

Deliberate misrepresentations of the Inquisition began during the Reformation, when Protestant factions breaking away from the Roman Church wanted to portray any activity of the Church in an unfavorable light. In the English-speaking world, such misrepresentation would have been concentrated on Spain, which coincided with a distancing of Spain as an ally due to the divorce case of Henry VIII and Catherine of Aragon. The highly influential *Book of Martyrs* by the Protestant historian John Foxe (ca. 1517–87) mentions "the extreme dealing and cruel ravening of these Catholic Inquisitors of Spain."[52] Other works by supposed escapees from the Inquisition in Spain led to the "Black Legend," the notion that the Spanish were horribly brutal, intolerant, and backward.[53] So the Spanish Inquisition, which was not directed by Rome at all, was inexorably intertwined with complaints about the pope. And once the Spanish Inquisition was brought into the argument, the Medieval Inquisition was included as well. Thus began the fiction of conflating the two Inquisitions as products of an intolerant Church.

Were one to single out a contemporary example of such prejudice and misinformation, one would have to look no further than Karen Armstrong, a popular historian who, while the darling of the History Channel and public television in the United States, is not taken seriously in the world of scholarly history. Yet in many ways she exemplifies the world of previous bias, writing in her book *Holy War* that the Inquisition was "one of the most evil of all Christian institutions...[a] noxious offspring of the Crusades...[an] iniquitous byword of orthodoxy...[and] a fanatical extreme."[54] She continues:

> Its methods were that "heretics" should be hunted out
> by a panel of inquisitors, who in the Catholic Church
> were usually the Dominicans....These bloodhounds of
> orthodoxy sniffed out the heretics of the community
> and people who held unacceptable views or were
> accused of "unchristian" practices were arrested and

flung into prison. There they would be tortured with unbelievable cruelty and made to "confess their crimes."...They were forced to confess that they worshipped the Devil or took part in monstrous sexual orgies; once they had been tortured beyond endurance, they had no further strength to deny the charges.... After confession, the heretics were handed over to the secular authorities and were then either hanged or burned at the stake.[55]

Fortunately, for scholars suspicious of such sensational language and outrageous claims, statistics exist for the Spanish Inquisition that categorize accusations according to seriousness of crime, and include the number of and nature of penalties, including those who were put to death and those hung in effigy. The work of Gustav Henningsen and John Tedeschi in compiling statistical information has been invaluable.[56] This information, as Rawlings points out, changes the landscape quite significantly:

First, the [Spanish] Inquisition was nowhere near as bloodthirsty and repressive an instrument of ideological control as commonly believed....Second, the pursuit of "Major Heresy" (as practiced by *conversos*, *moriscos*, Illuminists, and Lutherans) accounted for little more than 40% or two-fifths of inquisitorial activity between 1540 and 1700—the central period of the Inquisition's existence....Having all but eliminated the incidence of Major Heresy, the primary function of the Holy Office during the 1560s and 1570s became that of prosecuting the sins of popular ignorance and of instructing Spaniards on matters or morality and faith in accordance with the recommendations of the Council of Trent.[57]

Modern Jewish historians have discovered that, although one hundred persons would be sentenced to death in the Spanish

Inquisition, only one or two would be executed, and the rest were hung in effigy. The sensationalists of the Inquisitions—either Medieval or Spanish—need to admit this evidence and begin to give an honest assessment of what really happened. They will find, I believe, that what really happened was an amazingly humane legal process, begun with the idea of stopping the indiscriminate killing of lynch mobs and armies, and that is the foundation of our legal system today, flawed as it is.

Notes

The Crusades

1. The notion that there was an increase in violence against Christians immediately before 1095 has been largely discredited, but the previous violence and the perception of a renewal of violence were used by Pope Urban II as motivating factors in his call for a military pilgrimage to Jerusalem. See Christopher Tyerman, *God's War* (Cambridge, MA: Belknap Press, 2006), p. 81. This is disputed by Rodney Stark in his book *God's Battalions: The Case for the Crusades* (New York: HarperCollins, 2009), who has little patience for the idea that Muslim conquerors were "enlightened supporters of multiculturalism" (p. 29).

2. Philip Jenkins, *The Lost History of Christianity* (New York: HarperCollins, 2008), pp. 106–19.

3. If you were excommunicated, you could not take part in any Christian enterprise, from taking part in the Mass or sacraments, to going on crusade.

4. See Tyerman, *God's War*, pp. 84–85.

5. See Edward Peters, *The First Crusade* (Philadelphia: University of Pennsylvania Press, 1971), pp. xiv–xix.

6. Ibid., pp. xvii–xviii.

7. A recent movie, *The Way*, with Martin Sheen (2011) is about the pilgrimage route to Compostella and a compelling rationale for why such pilgrimages are taken.

8. See Peter Brown, *The Cult of the Saints* (Chicago: University of Chicago Press, 1982), and Marguerita Guarducci, *The Tomb of Peter* (New York: Hawthorn, 1960).

9. Whether these are "authentic" or genuine relics of the saints that they claim to be is another story. What is important here is that the people believed them to be authentic and venerated them as such. When the "Holy Lance," the lance that the Roman soldier Longinus was supposed to have thrust into the side of Christ at his crucifixion, was discov-

ered in Antioch by the crusaders during the First Crusade, it led to their recommitment to pressing on to Jerusalem.

10. In Patrick Geary, *Readings in Medieval History*, 4th ed. (Toronto: University of Toronto Press, 2010), p. 408. A popular belief among ordinary Christians was that Jews had caused the death of Christ and thus were liable to persecution.

11. I have heard this questioned by an historian who claimed that the horses ridden by the knights were not that large. I find this hard to believe, given the weight of the knight with his armor. A National Geographic expedition duplicated a trip from France to the Holy Land with a Belgian workhorse and a smaller horse, noting how travel was dictated by the larger horse. (Tim Severin, "Retracing the First Crusade," *National Geographic* 176, no. 3 [September 1989]: 326–65.)

12. This also needs to be nuanced, as Bohemond, one of the Norman commanders, was far more diplomatic on arriving in Constantinople than chroniclers have pictured him. Tyerman, *God's War*, p. 113. Much of our information about this episode comes from an account written by Anna Comnena, the emperor's daughter, which is uniformly critical of the westerners and written in hindsight. But her account, while valuable as a contemporary observation, has recently been reevaluated by scholars. Although Steven Runciman took her at face value (*A History of the Crusades*, Vol. 3 [Cambridge, UK: Cambridge University Press, 1951–54]), current historians question her objectivity.

13. We have his name as Firuz. Although some historians identify him as an Armenian Christian, it seems more probable that he was a convert to Islam (see Stark, *God's Battalions,* pp. 150–51). Bohemond had probably been negotiating with Christians inside the city for some time, but it is hardly likely that a Christian would be in charge of a defensive tower. The approach of Kerbogha's relief army made these negotiations and a breach of the walls more urgent. See Tyerman, *God's War*, p. 142.

14. See Tyerman, *God's War*, pp. 110–14, for an interesting read on Bohemond's reaction to victory.

15. Phillips thinks that more like 1,300 knights and 12,500 footmen were involved in the siege. (*Holy Warriors: A Modern History of the Crusades* [New York: Random House, 2009], p. 24.)

16. Zoe Oldenbourg, *The Crusades* (London: Weidenfeld & Nicolson, 1966), p. 133.

brought to Baghdad after the fall of Acre. He also mentions the chilling sight of watching nuns being marched off to harems. Ricoldo di Montecroce, *Peregrination en Terre Sainte et au Proche Orient* (Paris: Champion, 1997).

46. Tuchman, Barbara, *A Distant Mirror: The Calamitous Fourteenth Century* (New York: Knopf, 1978), pp. 538–63.

47. Madden, *A Concise History*, pp. 209–10, is insistent on this point, and it is generally accepted.

48. It is said that a new pastry was designed by Viennese bakers to celebrate this victory: the croissant, the crescent being the symbol of Turkey.

49. Runciman, *A History of the Crusades*, vol. 3, p. 480.

50. Fulcher of Chartres, "Account of the First Crusade," in Geary, *Readings in Medieval History*, p. 396.

51. Priests, even Western military chaplains, are not permitted to enter most Muslim countries. Churches are not allowed to be built, and public worship is not permitted. In fact, matters have gotten worse. With the advent of the Arab Spring of 2011, Christian enclaves are increasingly threatened by Islamic radicals.

52. Ayaan Hirsi Ali, "The Global War on Christians in the Muslim World," *Newsweek*, February 6, 2012. Available online at http://www. thedailybeast.com/newsweek/2012/02/05/ayaan-hirsi-ali-the-global-war-on-christians-in-the-muslim-world.html. Ms. Ali blames the Western media for being "reticent" on the subject of Islamic attacks on Christians in the Arab world, owing to their fear of provoking more violence and the success of Islamic lobbying groups such as the Organization of Islamic Cooperation, centered in Saudi Arabia, and the Council on American–Islamic Relations.

53. In 1988, an American Dominican sister was shot to death while walking with two Pakistani sisters in a public garden in Multan. The then-bishop of Multan, Bertrand Boland of the American Dominican Province of St. Joseph, said, "We did not know it then, but it was the beginning of Islamist violence against Christians" (Dominican Archives of the Province of St. Joseph, Providence College, Providence, RI, Pakistan File). In 2001, five Muslim extremists attacked a Protestant congregation using the church of St. Dominic in Bahawalpur, Pakistan, for a Sunday prayer service, spraying it indiscriminately with machine gun fire. Sixteen congregants, all of whom were Pakistanis, were killed.

The Inquisition

1. Edward Peters, *Inquisition* (New York: Free Press, 1988).

2. Benzion Netanyahu, *The Origins of the Spanish Inquisition in Fifteenth-Century Spain* (New York: Random House, 1995); Henry Kamen, *The Spanish Inquisition: A Historical Revision* (New Haven: Yale University Press, 1998); Helen Rawlings, *The Spanish Inquisition* (Oxford: Blackwell, 2006).

3. John O'Brien, *The Inquisition* (New York: Macmillan, 1973).

4. Herbert Grundmann, *Religious Movements in the Middle Ages* (Notre Dame, IN: Notre Dame University Press, 1995). This is translation of a classic, written in 1935. What is so refreshing about this work is that Grundmann treats all of the religious movements, whether orthodox or heretical, as part of a whole.

5. Alister McGrath, *Heresy: A History of Defending the Truth* (New York: HarperCollins, 2009), p. 208.

6. Ibid.

7. McGrath proceeds, not surprisingly, from his benign view of the Waldensian heresy to a discussion of the Reformation.

8. Manichaeism could thus be linked to Gnosticism, which preached a message of escape from our worldly chains.

9. Christopher Haigh is dismissive of the popularity of Lollardy (Wycliffites). He maintains that there were not many and that they were not necessarily vocal, but that later Protestants would make much of their presence. (*English Reformations* [New York: Oxford University Press, 1993]), pp. 51–55.

10. I think it instructive to see that, in order to meet new challenges from various historical forces, the Catholic Church would fraction from within—normally through the foundation of new religious orders—while the Protestant world would fraction from without, through the birth of new denominations.

11. Jonathan Riley-Smith, *The Crusades* (New Haven: Yale University Press, 2005), p. 165. The rest were sympathetic to the cause and promised to commit fully later in life. This division also occurred in historic Manicheism, where we find St. Augustine joining as a "believer" but not a fully committed Manichean.

12. Because the Albigensians did not believe that Christ was God, they can be distinguished from Christians who did. Since they also had

their own bishops, it is convenient (and accurate) to distinguish the one as an Albigensian bishop and the other as the Christian bishop. However, to avoid confusion in nomenclature, because the Albigensians regarded themselves as being "Christians" in a broad sense of the word, I distinguish them from "orthodox Christians."

13. Only five thousand people lived there, though this number may be somewhat higher owing to the presence of refugees. Generals often inflated the numbers of their victims in order to enhance their reputations and intimidate any towns in their paths.

14. J. N. D. Kelly, *The Dictionary of the Popes* (New York: Oxford University Press, 1986), pp. 176–77.

15. The Franciscans eventually had Dominic's style of government, with its centralized, pyramidal structure suffused with democracy at every level, imposed on them by the curia.

16. Riley-Smith, *Crusades*, p. 165.

17. The early life of the Prouille convent is not well documented, but we know that Dominic himself gave lectures on religious life to the nuns.

18. These would become known eventually as Poor Clares. They still exist today.

19. Henry VIII's case against Catherine of Aragon, for example, was an Inquisition trial.

20. O'Brien, *Inquisition*, p. 63.

21. The case of Anne Boleyn is a classic example. King Henry VIII needed to divorce her (she had not produced a male heir), so trumped-up charges were brought against her as having had sexual relations with court personnel, including her brother. These men were all tortured until they signed confessions, sometimes with offers of lenience in sentencing. They were then, with Anne Boleyn, all executed for treason.

22. John O'Malley, *The First Jesuits* (Cambridge, MA: Harvard University Press, 1993), pp. 310–12.

23. W. L. Wakefield, *Heresy, Crusade, and Inquisition in Southern France 1100–1250* (Berkeley: University of California Press, 1974), p. 71.

24. Peters, *Inquisition*, p. 57.

25. F. Merzbacher, "Witchcraft," *New Catholic Encyclopedia,* 2nd ed., vol. 14 (New York: Thomson Gale, 2003), p. 799.

26. Interestingly, a chapel Joan is thought to have frequented sits on the campus of Marquette University in Milwaukee, Wisconsin. It was discovered after World War I in the south of France by a brilliant young

French architect and archaeologist, who recognized its antiquity and made drawings of it. It got to the United States through Gertrude Gavin, the wife of James Hill, a railroad magnate, who purchased the chapel and had it dismantled and reconstructed on her estate in Jericho, Long Island. In 1962, the estate passed to Marc Rojtman, who donated it to Marquette University.

27. Excuses like these did not get you out of ecclesiastical penalties. People who pleaded ignorance usually got some sort of penalty, on the grounds that they should not have been ignorant.

28. The rivalries could become ferocious. When Bishop Oliver Plunkett made a decision over parish ownership in favor of the Dominicans, he was attacked by the Franciscans as being unfair. The three chief witnesses at his trial for treason were Franciscan friars.

29. In O'Brien, *The Inquisition*, p. 11.

30. Cullen Murphy, "Inquisitions: From Torquemada to the 'War on Terror,'" *Commonweal* (January 27, 2012): 13.

31. Pope John Paul II, *Tertio Millennio Adveniente*, no. 35 (cf. Vatican II's Document of Religious Freedom, *Dignitatis Humanae*, no. 1).

32. Kamen, *The Spanish Inquisition*, p. 23. He does this by projecting the percentage of Jews in cities of a known size onto cities of which the records are lost. Thus, if a city of forty thousand had a Jewish population of 8 percent, then Kamen will project that onto another comparable city with no records.

33. While the best modern scholarship focuses on the Jewish *conversos*, a surprisingly higher number of *moriscos* would be tried. In Aragon, for example, 942 Jewish converts were tried (not necessarily executed) between the years 1540 and 1700, while the number of Muslim converts tried was 7,472. In Castile the numbers are relatively equal (3,400 to 3,300). These numbers need to be qualified by noting that most of the activity directed against Jews (and presumably Muslims) took place before 1540. Prosecution of *moriscos* would increase in the seventeenth century (there remained a large number of *moriscos* because they were an essential part of the workforce) with the outbreak of several riots in Muslim neighborhoods.

34. Helen Rawlings, *The Spanish Inquisition*, p. 12.

35. Kamen, *The Spanish Inquisition*, p. 203.

36. Netanyahu, *The Origins of the Inquisition*; Haim Beinart, *Records of the Trials of the Spanish Inquisition in Ciudad Real, 1483–1485* (Jerusalem:

Israel National Academy of Science and Humanities, 1974);Yitzhak Baer, *A History of the Jews in Christian Spain* (Philadelphia: Jewish Publication Society of America, 1961).

37. In Rawlings, *The Spanish Inquisition*, p. 9.

38. Kamen, *The Spanish Inquisition*, pp. 98–102.

39. Rawlings, *The Spanish Inquisition*, p. 15.

40. Gustav Henningsen, "Spanish Archives and Historiography," in *The Inquisition in Early Modern Europe*, p. 56.

41. The book is practically a "paperback"—a small lightweight book in the possession of the Dominican Archives at Providence College. Unfortunately, during the writing of this book, it has been lost. I refer to it as Handbook for Inquisitors. The quotations are from several pages of photocopies in my possession, translated by Fr. Bede Shipps, OP.

42. *Handbook for Inquisitors*, Book I, chap. 7, p. 54.

43. Ibid., pp. 54–58.

44. Rawlings, *The Spanish Inquisition*, p. 136.

45. Kamen, *The Spanish Inquisition*, p. 203. The historian Henry Charles Lea (*A History of the Inquisition of Spain* [New York: Macmillan, 1922]) believed the original numbers and thus came up with his spectacularly inflated numbers of the dead.

46. In J. F. Frittelli et al., *Port and Maritime Security: Background and Issues* (New York: Novinka Books, 2003).

47. Kamen, *The Spanish Inquisition*, pp. 101–2.

48. Ibid., p. 161. O'Malley comments, "Few cases reveal so clearly the overheated religious atmosphere of Spain and Rome…or illustrate so dramatically the confusing and overlapping networks of jurisdictions, loyalties, and ecclesio-political policies and antagonisms within Catholicism" (*The First Jesuits*, p. 317).

49. O'Malley, *The First Jesuits*, p. 317.

50. Ibid., pp. 318–20. This same list had a "curious disclaimer" and included works by Thomas More and John Fisher (p. 319)!

51. See Maurice Finocchiaro, ed., *The Galileo Affair: A Documentary History* (Berkeley: University of California Press, 1989); Stillman Drake, trans., *Discoveries and Opinions of Galileo* (New York: Anchor Books, 1990).

52. In William Maltby, *The Black Legend in England: The Development of Anti-Spanish Sentiment 1558–1660* (Durham, NC: Duke University Press, 1971), p. 35.

53. See Rawlings, *The Spanish Inquisition*, pp. 4–5.

54. Karen Armstrong, *Holy War: The Crusades and Their Impact on Today's World* (New York: Doubleday, 1991), 456, 457, 459, 461.

55. Ibid., 457.

56. Gustav Henningsen and John Tedeschi, *The Inquisition in Early Modern Europe: Studies on Sources and Methods* (DeKalb: Northern Illinois University Press, 1986).

57. Rawlings, *The Spanish Inquisition*, p. 14.

Recommended Reading

A note on further reading: We are fortunate to live in an age in which there has been a revival of studies about both the Crusades and the Inquisition. For the past one hundred years, Crusade and Inquisition studies have been dominated by the names of Steven Runciman and Henry Charles Lea, whose reliance on original documents was groundbreaking but whose optimism about the results of such findings was sometimes misplaced. This happened generations earlier in Reformation studies, when Lord Acton predicted that one final definitive history of the English Reformation would be written that would never need to be replaced. Later historians, however, have found that documents need to be evaluated, weighed, and put in context, and that some conclusions reached needed to be supplanted. For example, the numbers of victims of the Inquisition listed in catalogs needed to be examined. With this in mind, I offer the following list as a compilation of the best of the most recent and readable scholarship.

The Crusades

Jenkins, Philip. *The Lost History of Christianity.* New York: Harper-Collins, 2008.
Jenkins is immensely popular. When describing the conditions in the Near East at the time of the early Church and into the period of the Crusades, he is superb. His work on Muslim–Christian relations is insightful.

Madden, Thomas F. *The New Concise History of the Crusades.* Lanham, MD: Rowman and Littlefield, 2005.
This book is solid, readable, and well documented.

Oldenbourg, Zoe. *The Crusades.* London: Weidenfeld & Nicolson, 1966.

Ms. Oldenbourg's book, considered a minor classic, covers only the first three crusades.

Peters, Edward, ed. *The First Crusade.* Philadelphia: University of Pennsylvania Press, 1971.

This is a collection of original documents, including eyewitness accounts of the First Crusade.

Riley-Smith, Jonathan. *The Crusades: A History.* New Haven: Yale University Press, 2005.

The work of Jonathan Riley-Smith on the Crusades is considered to be the best available in terms of completeness and readability. If I were to recommend a book on the Crusades, this (along with Madden's) is it.

Stark, Rodney, *God's Battalions: The Case for the Crusades.* New York: HarperOne, 2009.

The author tries to answer the question: How do you get fifty thousand men to walk three thousand miles—fighting a lot of the way—unless they are really angry about something? He supports the notion that the Turks have a lot to answer for in provoking the Westerners to go to war. Stark is more combative than most authors in defending the crusaders, but his work is solid.

Tyerman, Christopher. *God's War: A New History of the Crusades.* Cambridge, MA: Belknap Press, 2006.

This is a tome—more than a thousand pages in small print. It is more of a sourcebook than a history, although it is very readable. It is balanced and goes into *all* of the intrigues involved on both sides. He puts to rest a number of long-cherished but inaccurate assumptions about the Crusades. No stone is left unturned, which is to the book's detriment, I think. This is *not* the crusader version of Shelby Foote's masterful Civil War trilogy. This is a slog. If you are a student of the Crusades, it is a must.

The Inquisition

Kamen, Henry. *The Spanish Inquisition: A Historical Revision.* New Haven: Yale University Press, 1997.
This important book changed the prevalent thinking about the Spanish Inquisition.

O'Malley, John. *The First Jesuits.* Cambridge, MA: Harvard University Press, 1993.
The author is a first-rate historian and sheds much light on the Jesuit involvement in the Spanish Inquisition.

Peters, Edward. *Inquisition.* New York: Free Press, 1988.
This book is indispensable to Inquisition studies. Not only does the author give a balanced account of both the Medieval and Spanish Inquisitions, he documents the history of Inquisition "legends" and propaganda produced by Reformation and Enlightenment thinking, the artistic license taken by authors of fiction such as Dostoevsky and Poe, artists such as Goya, and musical composers such as Verdi. It is, if you want, a "complete guide" to the Inquisition.

Rawlings, Helen. *The Spanish Inquisition.* Malden MA: Blackwell, 2006.
This book is an excellent summary of the Spanish Inquisition and takes into account all of the latest research. The introduction provides a very helpful overview of the most recent findings by scholars as well, and the book contributes a balanced exposition of the Spanish Inquisition.